D0891696

# LIGHTEN
## OUR DARKNESS

# LIGHTEN
# OUR DARKNESS

*Discovering and celebrating Choral Evensong*

## SIMON REYNOLDS

DARTON·LONGMAN + TODD

First published in Great Britain in 2021 by
Darton, Longman and Todd Ltd
1 Spencer Court
140–142 Wandsworth High Street
London SW18 4JJ

ISBN: 978-0-232-53462-7

A catalogue record for this book is available from the British Library.

Designed and produced by Judy Linard
Printed and bound in Great Britain by Bell & Bain, Glasgow

In thanksgiving for the gifts of God in the
life and work of

JOHN GAVIN SCOTT
(1956 – 2015)

*Organ Scholar of St John's College, Cambridge*

*Assistant Organist of Southwark Cathedral*
*&*
*St Paul's Cathedral*

*Organist and Director of Music*
*St Paul's Cathedral*

*Organist and Director of Music*
*St Thomas Church, Fifth Avenue,*
*New York City*

# CONTENTS

7

Every man and woman in England has a birth-right. Walk into any cathedral at around about teatime, on just about any day of the week, and you will hear the most exquisite music beautifully sung. In the streets outside people are scrambling to get to the shops before they close, unaware perhaps that, behind this decorative medieval façade, a religious event of the most timeless beauty is about to take place. Choral Evensong is part of our cultural heritage... Something extremely precious, to be jealously guarded by those who sometimes need to be still, to think upon their divine creator, and to discover the immense capacities of the human soul.[1]

Joanna Trollope (1996)

# 1

# ECHOES OF ETERNITY
## *Evensong in Perspective*

OVER THE COURSE of the past 25 years, a quiet but persistent revolution has been taking place in English cathedrals, in some larger churches in major towns and cities, as well as the chapels of many university colleges. The numbers of people drawn by the distinctive musical character of their worship has risen significantly, with Choral Evensong becoming the locus of this persistent growth in the numbers of worshippers. A considerable number of these people are under 40 years of age; and many others have, until now, lived their lives on the edges of the Church – if not completely beyond it.

At a time when Western societies are becoming intentionally secular, when there is a discernible antagonism towards religious belief in the mass media, and the Church's own statistics are telling a story of overall decline in the parishes of the Church of England, increasing numbers of people are finding their way to worship in cathedrals and larger churches. In a society where the language and symbols of faith are widely misunderstood (if not alien) to most people, millions come to cathedrals – and many of them find their way to worship. People who would not otherwise be part of a local parish church feel they can claim a stake in these iconic cultural and religious landmarks.

Similar patterns are discernible in other places across

Europe. In a majority-Catholic country like France, where secularity (*Laïcité*) is the official stance of the state and the provision of ordained ministry and worship in parishes in many parts of the country is under considerable pressure, huge numbers have attended the Sunday evening Mass in Notre Dame Cathedral in Paris every week. Here, professional choral music (and the distinctive tradition of French organ music) was a notable feature before the devastating fire just before Easter 2019. It was always televised live – and continues to be so because the musicians and clergy of the Cathedral have found a temporary home in another of Paris's large churches, where the worship continues to draw large numbers of people across the age range. A similar pattern can be found at the Cathedral in Colögne, Northern Germany. Here, in addition to an extensive repertoire of European choral music to enrich the Roman Catholic liturgy, Choral Evensong in its English Anglican form takes place every Sunday evening, drawing large and diverse congregations. In other parts of Europe, monasteries are appealing to equally large numbers of people: not only to the space and silence they offer; but to their distinctive and disciplined pattern of worship, with its complex and captivating plainsong.

In the United States of America, cathedrals and parishes of the Episcopal Church (a sister Church of the Church of England) offer Choral Evensong regularly; as do several universities, that do not share the same denominational affiliation. They are discovering the appeal of worship that evolved, like Evensong, from the monastic tradition. The chapel of Duke University in Carolina (a Methodist foundation) offers a service based on Evensong several times each week; while Christ Church in New Haven, Connecticut, has choral worship based on the ancient monastic form of night prayer that is appealing to students from nearby Yale

University. These are just two examples of how students from a pressured academic environment are discovering a reflective space to be sustained by worship that has a transcendent and reflective quality. It reflects a growing pattern evident in those British colleges and universities whose chapels are home to accomplished choirs.

## STRANGE DIFFERENCE

Those who worship in cathedrals and other large churches are attracted by their strange, almost counter-cultural, ambience. Their large spaces allow you to be anonymous if you wish, as well as providing a space for stillness and silence. Their ability to combine liturgical stability and creativity with poise is another draw, especially where people are seeking an intelligent and imaginative expression of the Christian faith. Above all, it is their musical excellence that speaks to so many.

## GENEROUS SPACES

Choral Evensong is the act of worship that takes place on most evenings, in most Anglican cathedrals, on most days of the week. It is becoming recognised and valued as a precious gift. It is meeting the need that many people feel for a reflective space in their lives. Its fusion of music, words and silence seems to meet the desire of those who yearn for the time and space to ponder life's deepest questions – and to do so at their own pace. It is worship 'without strings'. There is a growing awareness that, because cathedrals 'do God' without the requirement to sign-up to some kind of commitment, you can easily slip in and out, without having to give an account of yourself to others. The beauty of the music, coupled to the scale of the architecture, makes the experience of worship in a cathedral quite unlike any other we know from daily life and work.

Cathedrals and their worship are not only places of cultural curiosity; they also enable people to face life's existential questions in a large and generous environment, against the backdrop of history and experience, which opens up a much broader perspective on the meaning of life and the things of God. In their own way, cathedrals and their worship witness to the belief that this is not a 'me-centred' – or even a human-centred – world. They also suggest that the dimension of mystery and the awe-inspiring can be compelling ways to explore faith.

In the late 1970s, when cathedrals and their worship were often regarded as something of a back-water in the Church of England, the journalist, Philip Toynbee, wrote of the impact of attending Choral Evensong with his wife on a Saturday afternoon in Peterborough Cathedral. His observations about the service – its seeming remoteness from life and his hope that what cathedrals offered would connect more imaginatively with the modern world in the future – is telling:

> … the dominant impression which remains is of a gracious, holy but esoteric ceremony being performed … massively isolated from the modern city outside by the wider spaces of the cathedral; by the close; by the little market-town which had already been long surrounded by an outer ring of railway-works and suburbs, and which was now being further enveloped by a new industrial sprawl. And yet we had not been only spectators of that deft performance; so far as each of us had found it possible, we had also been participants … For certainly we both belonged—wholly in spirit and largely in faith—with what was being celebrated in Peterborough Cathedral on that Saturday afternoon at the tail-end of the football season … But I doubt whether even the most fervent moderniser could believe that if

only the choir had been singing rock-and-roll, if only the lessons had proclaimed God the True Integration of Self, then the whole nave would have been filled with cheerful and loud-voiced participants, greatly to the detriment of the takings that afternoon by Peterborough United Football Club. It is absurd to pretend any longer that a jazzed-up liturgy ... will bring the multitude flocking back into our cathedrals and our parish churches ...[2]

Toynbee's reflections express the cultural perceptions of his time (not least the sense that Evensong was separate from 'real' life at a time when the decline in church-going was gathering pace). Nonetheless, his insights about how this ages-old pattern of formal prayer might still speak to people in a very different era will resonate with those who now value it, precisely because it *is* so different from the pace and pressure of much of contemporary life.

## NOT EASY

Cathedrals are characterised by the stability and continuity of their worshipping life. As well as being the seat of the bishop, they exist to offer worship: the daily Offices of Morning Prayer (sometimes called Matins) and Evening Prayer (Evensong); as well as the daily celebration of the Eucharist. The worship offered in cathedrals is predominantly structured, hierarchical, formalised and punctuated by a high level of musical and linguistic sophistication. It provides a framework in which music, architecture and language offer space to recover a true sense of our humanity before God. It is not an immediately accessible form of worship. It makes mental and cultural demands on those encounter it – not least through its music. It has to be worked at if it is to become a familiar and natural feature of the spiritual landscape. As John

Drury, a former Dean of King's College, Cambridge, has observed:

> We need to do two things in order to enter into the spirit of these services. First, we have to be patient and relaxed enough to allow a long tradition to have its say. Then we should allow our own thoughts and feelings to become closer to us than life outside usually allows. These two things are not separate. In the tradition there are, along with what is strange, strong expressions of our basic feelings about ourselves and God. And it is precisely the cool and ancient order of the services which gives us a space and a frame, as well as cues, for reflections on our regrets, hopes and gratitudes. The best analogy of this is a relationship of love. There, as here, we find ourselves by attending to another. So we learn here a little of what we need and enjoy everywhere.[3]

This may not seem immediately attractive to contemporary cultural expectations. In a world of instant digital communication, where most people are attached in some way to their mobile 'phone while they are awake, and shorter attention spans co-exist with the easy availability of fast food, giving sustained attention to any form of artistic endeavour is testing. We tend to expect speed and immediacy as the norm, and may even resent the need to wait for anything at all. For some, even the long-term commitment of an intimate relationship with another person can be challenging.

Choral Evensong is not a quick fix. It does not appear to offer concessions to those for whom the language, beliefs and symbols of Christianity are unfamiliar or unknown. There is no doubt that cathedrals are committed to being places of welcome, where a sense of community is flourishing, along with the language of justice and a concern for the wider world. But Choral Evensong is not obviously 'user friendly' or 'accessible' in the way this is often understood in many local parish churches – and some observed attempts to make it so have usually diminished rather than enhanced its appeal. Yet cathedrals and college chapels continue to be attractive as places of worship – particularly for those who have not always considered themselves 'religious'. This may be because, in a world of rolling 24-hour news, where technological advances mean that many people struggle to maintain boundaries between work and down-time, there is a growing need for places of stillness, even silence and sanctuary. Cathedrals and their worship offer pools of refreshment and reflection. They invite us to step aside from the relentless drive of much modern living: not to escape so much as to be able to discover how to begin making sense of the demands and opportunities of life with greater clarity and insight. It may enable us to accept that there is much more to our lives than our distracted minds and tired bodies: we are much more than mere cogs in the vast machinery of global economic and commercial productivity. As a Christian hermit of the fourth century once suggested, anyone who has a heart can be saved. That is just one way of suggesting that, whatever our response may be to the worship being offered at this present moment, it is enough. We are not being asked for more than we can give or commit to with integrity.

## EMERGING PATTERNS

The growth being experienced by cathedrals, and other places where Choral Evensong is offered, is part of a much wider pattern of changing religious activity across Europe. As the cultural influence of the historic churches continues to decline, growing numbers of people are discovering that they want to speak about what they believe, what brings them fulfilment, and how the need for a 'spiritual dimension' to life can be met. The growth in well-being retreats offered by non-religious organisations, as well as the tendency to take profound questions about the meaning of life to medical (rather than religious) professionals, corroborates this to a large extent. Meanwhile, fewer people express a need to belong to the institutional Church at a local level. This is particularly the case where belonging to the Church is synonymous with signing-up to an organisation, where matters of belief and lifestyle are perceived as being tightly defined, and where making commitments of time, skills and energy are expected. Political parties, sports clubs, as well as traditional youth organisations (such as Scouting and Guiding), report similar trends.

Nonetheless, some traditional patterns of Christianity seem to be nourishing the longings some people feel once more about life, about what makes them human and, ultimately, a latent fascination with the things of God. In an aggressively secular culture like contemporary Britain, where every sphere of life seems to be governed by productivity targets, commercial outcomes and raw profit, increasing numbers of people are seeking a means of passive resistance: by searching for space to ponder life's mysteries; or to find a place of sanctuary. However they express it, many people are asking if they have a 'soul' – and how it can be nourished and enlarged.

## SURPRISING

This partly explains the rediscovery of pilgrimage, whether this is along one of the traditional routes (from Winchester to Canterbury or the *Camino* from France to Santiago de Compostela in Northern Spain) or along routes of peoples' own devising. Traditional pilgrimage centres, such as Walsingham, Iona and Lindisfarne, as well as many cathedrals that house shrines to saints, such as Durham and Chichester, are inviting wider attention and reporting increased numbers of visitors. Very often, the distinction between tourists and pilgrims is hard to delineate. Pilgrimage offers space for reflection, a slower pace, the opportunity to encounter difference, and the prospect of being surprised by what is new and unexpected. It also offers a way of engaging with the history and practice of Christianity, especially for those who might not otherwise be attracted to their local churches.

Yet pilgrimage is not easy. It can be physically, spiritually and mentally demanding. The geographical and psychological terrain which pilgrims negotiate can be tough and uncompromising. It is an experience that can be transformative and costly in equal measure. Whether pilgrims claim a religious identity or not, whether prayer (in its commonly understood definitions) accompanies their journey, whether the goal of their journey is a recognised holy place or not; the experience of pilgrimage takes people 'somewhere else'. It is an encounter with difference – and that difference invariably proves to be enlarging, even life-changing.

Others have discovered the value and potential of monastic communities, with their emphasis on the balance between work, silence, prayer and community interdependence. In France, for example, where Roman Catholicism is in steep decline in local parishes, many forms of monasticism are vibrant and growing. Across Europe, Catholic and Reformed churches are experiencing similar developments – not least in what might be called the 'new' monastic movements. Examples of these include the ecumenical monastic community at Taizé in Burgundy (founded by a Swiss Reformed pastor in 1948); the Chemin Neuf movement (a Roman Catholic community founded in Lyon in the early 1970s with an ecumenical outlook);

and in the evolution of traditional monastic communities, such as the Anglican Society of St Francis at Hilfield in Dorset, where professed friars live alongside single people and families seeking to live sustainably and peacefully in harmony with creation. In many of the 'new' monastic communities across Europe, those who belong to them do an ordinary day's work; but commit themselves to living in community with a rule of life centred around set times of daily prayer and caring for specific groups of people (the homeless, the disabled or refugees, for example). Examples can be found at La Chaise Dieu, deep in the French Massif Central; in Amsterdam's 'Red Light' district; as well as Peckham in South London.

## NEVER ALONE

Choral Evensong can be seen as part of this momentum of pilgrimage and a monastic way of prayer. Not only did Evensong evolve from the monastic pattern of daily prayer; it continues to offer a stable, reliable and regular pattern of daily worship. In one sense, it makes few demands because it is simply given. It usually happens at a time when people are heading home from work, or have finished school or shopping, visiting people in hospital, a care home or prison, when the axis of the day begins to turn from light to darkness. It offers a space into which the concerns, failures and achievements of the day can be brought into the wide and generous orbit of the Church's worship.

Whether a person goes to Evensong alone, or with others, it is never an isolated activity. Of course, there are other people present – not least the choir, clergy and others whose task it is organise and offer this worship. But there is a much wider – and deeper – dimension to this sense of being part of something greater than oneself – or even the present moment. This is significant at a time when increasing numbers of people under the age of 35 are more likely to experience loneliness than those over the age of 55.

At one level, Evensong embodies a strong sense of continuity. The words being said and sung, and the basic shape of the service, has been part of Christian experience from a very early moment in our history. It takes us back to our roots in the Jewish faith of Jesus and his followers. At another level, the same (or very similar) words are being said or sung in many other places, at around the same time, all over the world: not simply in other cathedrals with glorious music; but by small groups and isolated individuals; in small country churches, hospitals and immigration centres, in affluent societies or in places of grinding poverty and brutal persecution. The worship in which we are involved inescapably binds us to other people, other cultures and other times.

This is an act of worship that gently reminds us that, while each of us is infinitely precious to God, as twenty-first century people we are not the centre of the universe. Others have been nourished and enlarged by this worship long before us – and will continue to do so long after our lives on earth have ended. Evensong may be happening at a specific time and in a particular place, here and now; but we are inescapably part of the praying of countless millions of unknown and unknowable people with whom we share this worshipping experience across time and space. This is why it is natural to speak of Evensong as part of the *Church's* worship, rather than simply being an act of personal devotion. This is worship that takes us out of ourselves and challenges our self-referential tendencies. It invites us to journey into unfamiliar territory, to discover the wider horizons of life, history and faith, and to acknowledge that we share this fragile planet with others.

# EXPANSIVE MUSIC

The music that is integral to Choral Evensong is an obvious way of accentuating the sense of continuity underscoring this act of worship. Unless a piece of music happens to be receiving its first performance, the music that you will hear has been sung – and heard – many times before: possibly for centuries. It is both inspiring and humbling to know that we are not the first (and will not be the last) people for whom this music has accompanied and articulated our longing, hope and gratitude. Its regular repetition in many different places absorbs the prayers of countless generations of people.

I have often been most acutely aware of this on a Friday, when the service is sparser in feel (and traditionally sung without organ accompaniment) to recall the day of the crucifixion. It is a day when much of the music tends to come from the Medieval and Tudor periods, and may also include plainsong – one of the earliest known forms of music used in Christian worship. It seems to amplify the architectural space in which the worship takes place (in a cathedral dating from the Middle Ages or earlier), where the music, as well as aspects of the worshipping environment, may be contemporaneous. Even in a twentieth-century cathedral, such as Coventry or Liverpool, there is a keen sense that music from an earlier period is gently challenging the tendency to imagine that Christian worship is purely of the present moment (or within living memory). Similarly, the presence of contemporary music in an ancient cathedral, especially its more angular dissonance, serves as a reminder that the worship being offered, although in beautiful and ancient surroundings, is not remote from the anguished and urgent realities of the present day. One of the ways music works its mysterious power in worship is to insist that reality is much more than what we may know or understand at this moment. Not only can it invite us to ponder the essential truth about our place in this vast and complex universe; it also opens a window through which we can glimpse the endless possibilities of eternity.

Understood in this way, music in Christian worship performs, in John Keats' words, 'A priest-like task'. If we will let it, music can hold up an undistorted mirror to the human condition. Harmony and dissonance, rhythm and stillness, as well as major and minor keys, provide their own commentary on the exigencies of life. It challenges us to embrace the whole world with all its dazzling beauty, all its devastating pain, and all its horrific injustice. When words, architecture and music come together in a large worshipping space like a cathedral, it can invite worshippers to inhabit a place to face reality at its most intense, and to be drawn more deeply into the orbit of God's redeeming and healing love.

## A GIFT THAT KEEPS GIVING

Choral Evensong is not a modern invention designed to attract more people into church and stem the momentum of decline. It has evolved over many centuries. Although several elements take us back to the worshipping experience of Jesus in the Jewish faith, the current framework of the service was largely fixed in the mid-sixteenth century (with some minor revisions over the course of the next century or so). After the great religious and political upheaval of the Reformation, which gave birth to new forms of Christian worship across Europe during the sixteenth century, Evensong was one of the services that adapted the worship of the monasteries for ordinary people and their clergy to use together. In that sense, it simply perpetuates what the Church has always done, without any attempt to make it more relevant, to adapt it to meet today's cultural expectations, or to overlay it with endless explanation that may diminish its impact. Its language belongs more to the world of Shakespeare than Twitter. Some of the music may not be 'easy listening.' The readings from Jewish and Christian scriptures expose us to 'another country' in the ancient near-East and parts of the Mediterranean. This is a world we cannot easily know, where human rights, antibiotics and air travel were unimaginable.

Notwithstanding its rooting in the past, Choral Evensong seems to attract and invite today precisely because it is a gift – and a gift that demands little or nothing in return. As part of the diverse 'mixed economy' of worship in the Church of England, people can stumble upon it unexpectedly, or grow in familiarity after an initial and hesitant encounter. Anyone attending Evensong in a cathedral or large church can be confident that they will not be quizzed about their motives and beliefs, or pressured to leave their contact details. The fact that it is possible to worship with a large degree of anonymity, and not be expected to conform to a pre-determined view of what it means to belong to the Church, is part of the attraction for many people.

Another aspect of Choral Evensong that makes it attractive is that, on the whole, it happens on most days of the week, rather than being a Sunday-only occasion. Whilst the 'traditional' Sunday may persist in many countries across the European mainland, it tends to be much more fragmented in the Anglo-Saxon world. Not only do many (especially younger) people feel they must work on Sundays; but the competing demands of sporting activities, as well as the complexities that surround life for divorced or separated parents, or the relentless demands of working in the gig economy with zero-hours contracts, means that worship on Sundays can be problematic – if not impossible – for many people. Being able to slip into worship, as the working or learning day is ending, can be as liberating as it is convenient.

## BEING AT HOME

Once we arrive and take our seat for Evensong, little else is asked of us. We are not expected to do – or even say – very much. Although the service has a dialogical character, most obviously between priest and choir, and (especially during the Psalms) between the two sides of the choir, that dialogue is one that allows us to find our own level of involvement. Evensong is an act of worship that invites rather than compels. It allows us to gradually feel at home in its centuries-old contours, and to bring to it our own deeply felt needs and persistent hopes. It also allows us to catch the echoes and resonances of God speaking through the beauty of what our senses receive: to be comforted and challenged by the words and music; and encouraged to respond without specifying what that response must be. Our freedom to simply *be* is one of the outcomes of the choir, clergy and others leading the worship by using their gifts and skills, often after many years of disciplined study and practice, to carry our hopes, our burdens and our prayers.

## DEEPLY INVOLVED

On the surface, we may seem only passive onlookers of what is being said and sung; but we are never excluded. This is not about being entertained: it is participation by giving our attention to the creativity of others, and being invited to involve ourselves in the spiritual energy they are evoking and generating. In many respects, it is a level of participation that can be just as passionate as if we were singing or speaking ourselves. It is the kind of participation that can be experienced at a sporting event such as a football match; or when we are completely captivated by a work of art, or another person's face. As the former Archbishop of Canterbury, Rowan Williams (once a cathedral canon himself) has suggested, this can allow us to grasp what encountering God might be like when we give our complete attention to someone (or something) beyond ourselves, as we inhabit:

> ...the moment of acknowledged conviction, shared by two people, that each is accepted, given time and room, treated not as an object of desire alone, but as a focus of fascination and attention.[4]

Understood in this way, we may find that we are becoming enveloped by the worship, immersed in the glory of the God who created us out of love to reflect that same glory. Choral Evensong is worship that respects the integrity and uniqueness of each person, without ever coercing us to reinvent ourselves or adopt a new identity. In the space we are given to reflect, receive and respond, we may find that our awareness of God is being deepened with our longing to become part of the vast ocean of prayer that the Church offers in every time and place, as we begin to see the world and other people with the wisdom and compassion that is at the heart of God's own being.

# 2
# ROOTS, SHAPE
# AND FLOW
## *Evensong Unwrapped*

EVENSONG IS THE popular name given to the sung service of Evening Prayer that the Church of England (and other churches of the worldwide Anglican Communion) has offered towards the close of the day since the publication of the first *Book of Common Prayer* in 1549. However, this date is just one milestone on the long journey of discovering how this service took the form that is widely used today. If we have some understanding of its history, and how its words and music have evolved over time, it may help to see how our own experience of the service today can be part of its developing story.

## THE RHYTHM OF TIME
When Christianity emerged from its Jewish roots in the second half of the first century of the Christian Era (CE), the earliest Christian communities broadly continued with the worship they had known from the synagogue. In particular, they would have followed the Jewish custom of marking time at significant moments of each day: in the morning; in the middle of the day; and at evening. These times of prayer included psalms and readings from the Bible.

27

As Christianity began to grow as a distinctive movement, and spread widely beyond its native soil in Israel/Palestine, it carried this pattern of worship into the new communities it formed around the Middle East and Eastern Mediterranean – not least because some of them would have been part of existing Jewish diaspora groups.

After the conversion of the Roman Emperor Constantine (312 CE), when Christian worship took on a more public character after several centuries of hostility and persecution, the set times of daily prayer became formal, public acts of worship, in contrast to the subversive and covert activity it had once been. In particular, there was a time of prayer in the morning that focussed on the cross, and a celebration in the evening, with its emphasis on Christ as the light of the world. It is from around this time that one of the earliest Christian hymns originates, written for the lighting of lamps at the beginning of Evening Prayer. It continues to be used today, notably in an anthem by Charles Wood (1866-1926):

> Hail, gladdening Light, of his pure glory poured
> Who is the immortal Father, heavenly, blest,
> Holiest of holies, Jesus Christ our Lord!
>
> Now we are come to the sun's hour of rest;
> The lights of evening round us shine;
> We hymn the Father, Son, and Holy Spirit divine!
>
> Worthiest art thou at all times to be sung
> With undefiled tongue,
> Son of our God, Giver of life, alone:
> Therefore in all the world
> Thy glories, Lord, they own.[5]

These services of prayer and praise retained a broadly Jewish character, with readings from the Bible, psalms, and prayers that praised God for his work in creation. By the Fourth century CE, Christian belief and practice had developed considerably in moving away from its Jewish origins. Consequently, the work of God in creation was linked to the salvation of the world accomplished in the death and resurrection of Jesus Christ. The psalms, in particular, were often chosen to echo and resonate with a Christian understanding of salvation.[6] These were often popular times of worship in major cities, at which the local bishop presided, where a combination of words, symbols and music nurtured the prayer (and fed the spiritual imagination) of early Christian communities.

## A PLACE APART

As Christianity emerged from persecution to become the official religion of the Roman Empire in the early part of the fourth century, a movement of protest began to emerge. A growing number of men and women became dissatisfied by how easily Christianity seemed to identify with the imperial power of the state. They began withdrawing from the new-found comfort and prosperity of urban life, and went to live in poverty and isolation in the deserts of Egypt, Israel/Palestine, Syria and (what is now) Turkey.

While some of these men and women (often referred to as the Desert Fathers and Mothers) lived a solitary life as hermits; many of them gathered for prayer at various times of the day and night. The frequency of these times of prayer, centred on reciting psalms, increased. Over time, this began to develop into a more complex pattern, distinct from the popular forms of prayer in the morning and evening observed by Christians living in urban settings. In certain respects, these early Christians, who embraced the intensity of life of the desert, laid the foundations for the monastic communities that flourished more widely over the following millennium.

With the eventual collapse of the Roman Empire towards the end of the fifth century CE, and the economic upheaval and tribal feuding that followed, the stable institutions of civil society in the former Empire were in a state of collapse. Within the Church, not all of the disputes to settle and agree the nature of the Christian faith had been finally resolved. Amid this political and cultural dysfunction, the monasteries emerged as a civilising influence by offering an alternative pattern of social cohesion, with their focus on prayer, work, stability and community interdependence. Various personalities were crucial in forging this pattern of Christian living from the sixth century CE onwards, notably Benedict of Nursia (*c.* 480-547). Benedict's *Rule* provided the foundation for monastic life over the course of the next millennium and beyond, with each day carefully punctuated by times of worship, beginning before daybreak and ending at nightfall. The seven services of the monastic day retained the core character of singing psalms and hearing readings from the Bible, with an emphasis on praise for God's work in creation and the redeeming love of Christ.

One of the consequences of the growth in monastic life is that the popular forms of prayer in the morning and evening, celebrated by clergy and people together, developed in the Western world into something more complex, reserved for the professional clergy and those who belonged to monastic communities. The pattern of prayer in the monasteries each day meant that, apart from worshipping together at the Eucharist, clergy and lay people no longer shared a common form of daily prayer.

# SHATTERING DIVISIONS

During the late Middle Ages, England was known as the 'Land of the Benedictines' because so many monastic communities following the *Rule of St Benedict* (as it became known) were established in every part of the country. Some of them are now cathedrals of the Church of England: among them Durham, Coventry, Ely, Norwich, Winchester and Worcester; along with major churches such as the abbeys at Bath, Tewkesbury and Westminster. In total, there were around 900 monasteries in the British Isles.

As the religious and political upheaval that triggered the Reformation across Europe in the sixteenth century began to take hold in the British Isles during the reign of Henry VIII, many aspects of Christian belief and practice that had evolved over the previous millennium, were dismantled. The monasteries were a conspicuous casualty. Over the course of five years, beginning in 1536, the monastic communities of England, Wales and Ireland were disbanded and broken up. Their lands and assets were confiscated by the Crown, and much of the proceeds used to finance the King's military campaigns. Some of these great monastic churches became cathedrals following the reorganisation of the English Church and the creation of new dioceses in the early 1540s (e.g. Chester, Gloucester and Peterborough). Some also became parish churches. Most fell into ruin and their remains can be seen in many places across the country (e.g. Rievaulx in Yorkshire, Tintern near the Welsh border, and Walsingham in Norfolk).

After the death of Henry VIII and the succession of Edward VI in 1547, the impact of the Reformation began to be more keenly felt through the changing nature of the Church's worship, resulting in the first *Book of Common Prayer* in 1549. This was the first of many editions of what has popularly become known as 'The Prayer Book' that would be published over the subsequent century and more, to express how the evolving theology of the Reformation would be expressed in the English Church. The revision of 1662, following the restoration of the monarchy after the Civil War, remains the statutory Prayer Book of the Church of England. This provides the form of Choral Evensong used in cathedrals and other churches and chapels today.

## RADICAL SIMPLICITY

One of the enduring outcomes of the *Book of Common Prayer* was not only the change from Latin to English as the language of worship, along with the simplification of much of the ceremonial and symbolism, but the emphasis on *common prayer*. It recovered the principle of twice-daily prayer, in the morning and evening, shared by clergy and people together that had been a feature of Christian worship in earlier centuries.

Thomas Cranmer (1489-1556), who was Archbishop of Canterbury during the reign of Edward VI (and later martyred during the reign of Queen Mary) is considered to be the architect of the *Book of Common Prayer*. Significantly, Cranmer had been educated at Jesus College, Cambridge, which had formerly been the Benedictine Priory of St Radegund, where the monastic pattern of worship would have been central to its life. His Prayer Book was not only a book of prayers and services; it also contains the doctrinal framework for the Church of England's distinctive identity. It is often said that, if you want to know what the Church of England believes, you will find it between the covers of the *Book of Common Prayer*. In that sense, worship in the Church of England reflects a Latin motto dating from the early fifth century CE, *Lex orandi lex credendi* (the law of praying forms the law of believing).[7]

Cranmer's re-working of the elaborate Medieval worship of the monasteries into the two daily services of Morning and Evening prayer was particularly effective. Not only do these services retain the fundamental character of the monastic services, with their emphasis on the psalms and the reading of the Bible; they would also have been recognised by the earliest Christians emerging from their Jewish roots.

Morning Prayer (common called 'Matins') is, broadly, a fusion of the Medieval services of Matins and Lauds. The first took place in the early morning before daybreak; and the second at sunrise. Evening Prayer (commonly called 'Evensong') combined the evening service of Vespers and the last service of the day, Compline, which took place just before the community went to sleep.

## ENDURING MUSIC

Unlike other parts of Europe, England retained its choral foundations in cathedrals and colleges following the Reformation, with only a brief suspension during the Commonwealth (1649-1660). English composers, such as Christopher Tye (c.1505-72), John Sheppard (1515-58) and Thomas Tallis (c.1505-85), who had composed gloriously florid music for the Latin worship of the Medieval Church, began composing simpler music for the worship of the Prayer Book that gave the words greater clarity. Their successors, including William Byrd (c.1540-1623), Orlando Gibbons (1583-1625) and Thomas Tomkins (1572-1656) continued to develop this distinctive tradition; with John Blow (1649-1708), Henry Purcell (1659-95) and their contemporaries renewing the tradition after the restoration of the monarchy in the mid-seventeenth century.

# RENEWAL AND REFORM

Although there are well-chronicled accounts of apathy and negligence overshadowing the worship and music of English cathedrals during the late-eighteenth and early-nineteenth centuries, the choral tradition continued. After the Tractarian revival that gained momentum in the second half of the nineteenth century, where a renewed interest in the pre-Reformation traditions of worship flourished (not least in the universities of Oxford and Cambridge where most clergy were educated), a greater desire for order and dignity in worship became widespread. The tradition of choral services found in cathedrals and college chapels began to develop in parish churches as new clergy took up parochial appointments. Bands of local musicians, who had played psalms and hymns from the West galleries in churches, were replaced by organs, and by choirs wearing cassocks and surplices, as they mostly do today. The great Tractarian reformer, Walter Farqhar Hook (1798-1875), established the first robed choir in a Church of England parish church since the Reformation during his time as Vicar of Leeds, where (until 2016) Leeds Minster was the only parish church in England to maintain daily Choral Evensong. Hook's stated intention was to bring the beauty of holiness to the heart of the squalor and deprivation that was a consequence of the Industrial Revolution and mass migration into Northern cities at that time.

In essence, the way Choral Evensong is ordered in cathedrals, churches and chapels today is a reflection of this late nineteenth-century pattern, with its disciplined order and high quality of singing. The organist and composer Samuel Sebastian Wesley (1810-76), whom Hook had brought to Leeds in 1842 before he moved on to Winchester, was a key personality in raising standards after the malaise of earlier generations. Charles Villiers Stanford (1852-1924), who was organist of Trinity College, Cambridge, and later a professor at the Royal College of Music, set a new standard in composing music that rejected the hollow sentimentality of previous decades by paying greater attention to musical form. As a teacher, his influence was considerable. Many of his pupils are familiar names from the world of choral music, including Ralph Vaughan Williams (1875-1958) and Herbert Howells (1892-1983), who enriched the tradition with the quality and originality of their compositions. Howells, in particular, wrote a series of specially-tailored settings of the canticles that form the core of Evensong for many English cathedrals and college chapels. He is the composer from this generation whose music is most likely to be heard regularly today.

## FRESH EXPRESSIONS

The period after the Second World War was an especially fertile era for the composition of new and original music for cathedral worship. Benjamin Britten (1913-1976), Kenneth Leighton (1929-1989), Peter Maxwell-Davies (1934-2016), William Mathias (1934-1992), John Tavener (1944-2013) and Jonathan Harvey (1939-2012) contributed originality and a distinctive 'voice' to the development of the choral tradition in cathedrals and chapels, as well as writing symphonies, concertos and chamber music. Alongside these composers, many cathedral organists of the twentieth century were (and are) skilled and original composers, and their music continues to be heard regularly, notably three organists of York Minster, Edward Bairstow (1874-1946), Francis Jackson (b. 1917) and Philip Moore (b. 1943).

In so many ways, the standards of music we enjoy in cathedrals, chapels and some other churches today have never been higher and can be enjoyed widely through the availability of recordings and webcasts. Today, there is no shortage of serious composers willing to write new music for cathedral and church choirs, including Stephen Paulus (b. 1946), Judith Bingham (b. 1952), Judith Weir (b. 1954), Geraint Lewis (b. 1958), Jonathan Dove (b. 1959), James MacMillan (b 1961), Roxanna Panufnik (b. 1968), Ēriks Ešenvalds (b. 1977), Matthew Martin (b. 1976) and David Bednall (b. 1979). A significant factor in encouraging this impulse has been the enduring influence of Stephen Cleobury (1948-2019), Director of Music at King's College, Cambridge from 1982-2019. His policy of commissioning a new carol from a serious contemporary composer for the Festival of Nine Lessons and Carols each year has been crucial in ensuring that liturgical choral music has been a mainstream activity for composers who are not otherwise considered as 'church' composers. Their creativity and artistry continues to renew the tradition and bring a fresh perspective to a unique and precious act of worship that has sustained, consoled and inspired countless millions of people.

# CHORAL EVENSONG AT A GLANCE

This has only been a hurried telling of the much longer and detailed story of how Choral Evensong has been handed on to the present generation of worshippers – many of whom may be discovering it for the first time.

To round-off this fast gallop across the terrain, I have sketched a 'map' of Choral Evensong. If this way of worship is new to you, or even if you have been familiar with it for much of your life, it may be helpful in providing an overview of the various components of the service and illustrating how they fit together.

In subsequent chapters, we will explore these various components in more detail.

In what follows, the essential parts of the service are

in **bold** type. Those elements of the service that are either optional, or which may not happen on some days during the week, are in plain type. I have assumed that the service will reflect the widespread practice of most English cathedrals and chapels today, rather than following strictly the order of service in the 1662 *Book of Common Prayer*.

# THE PREPARATION

INTROIT

>*In some places, Choral Evensong begins with the choir singing a short anthem to set the tone of the service, or to provide seasonal emphasis to the worship that it about to take place. An introit may only be sung on Sundays or major festivals to heighten the significance of the day. In some places it may not feature at all.*

PENITENTIAL INTRODUCTION

>*These prayers, which express sorrow for the fears and failures of our lives, and the assurance of God's endless capacity to forgive all who turn to him in faith, may take place on a Friday and at weekends. Historically, an act of penitence was rarely part of Morning and Evening Prayer, and did not feature in the first Prayer Book of 1549. Prayers of penitence were first introduced in the revision of 1553.*

**OPENING RESPONSES**

>This is most likely to be where Choral Evensong begins on most days, as the priest and choir call on God at the start of worship. The first two responses are words from the Psalms, and have been the opening words of daily prayer for many centuries.

They are followed by an acclamation in praise of God's Trinitarian character (which will be repeated several more times in the course of the service).

# HEARING & RESPONDING TO THE WORD OF GOD

**PSALMS**

Each day, a psalm or several psalms are sung. They are the backbone of the service, and have been a feature of Christian daily prayer from the beginning. They are part of the Hebrew Bible and are the most obvious way in which our worship expresses our Jewish roots. The *Book of Common Prayer* has a system for dividing the psalms up into daily portions, so that they are all sung over the course of a month at Morning and Evening Prayer. Many cathedrals and chapels still follow this scheme. Others use more recent schemes.

**FIRST LESSON**

The first of two readings from the Bible comes from the *Tanekh*, the Hebrew Bible (what Christians call the 'Old Testament'); or from the so-called 'Deutero-Canonical' books (often called the Apocrypha). Like the psalms, there is a scheme for reading portions of the Bible in worship.

HYMN

*Particularly on major festivals and saints' days, a short hymn may be sung at this point. This was never a feature of the* Book of Common Prayer *and its inclusion reflects a practice that developed before the Middle Ages, when a hymn would be sung to mark the time of day or season*

*of the year. In some places, this hymn is sung earlier in*
*the service, before the psalms begin.*

## MAGNIFICAT

This is the first of the two canticles (or songs) that are an unchanging feature of Choral Evensong. It comes from the first chapter of the Gospel according to Luke. It is often called the 'Song of Mary' to reflect its setting the Gospel, as Mary the mother of Jesus rejoices with her cousin, Elizabeth, as they both prepare to give birth following an angelic visit.

## SECOND LESSON

The second of two readings from the Bible comes from the Christian scriptures (the New Testament): from one of the Gospels, that record the words and deeds of Jesus; or from one of the letters written to early Christian communities, from the accounts of the early Christian mission in Acts, or (towards the end of the year especially) the visions recorded in the book of Revelation.

## NUNC DIMITTIS

The second of the two canticles that are a fixed element in the service also comes from the Gospel according to Luke. Popularly known as the 'Song of Simeon' it is the outpouring of praise and relief by an old man, now near the moment of death, who has waited a lifetime to see the promised Saviour, the infant Christ in his mother's arms.

## APOSTLES CREED

One of the definitive statements of Christian belief is recited (or intoned by the choir) as response to hearing the scriptures. As an expression of the corporate (or catholic) identity of the Church, it recalls one of the defining moments in the long history of the development of Christian belief.

# THE PRAYER OF THE CHURCH

## LESSER LITANY, LORD'S PRAYER, PRECES & COLLECTS

This is another element of Evensong that is unchanging from day to day. Beginning with an acknowledgement of our need for mercy, then followed by the prayer Jesus taught his followers to use, the priest and choir then offers a sequence of short prayers (*Preces* in Latin). They express our dependence on God, both for our own well-being and the stability of the world. It concludes with three formal prayers (Collects). The first changes weekly (or daily on festivals); the last two are fixed throughout the year.

## ANTHEM

This is often the principal musical opportunity to articulate joy or sorrow, hope or lament; or to emphasise the seasonal character of the worship. It offers worshippers a space to become absorbed in the music that expresses and enlarges the words being sung. It can also be a time when the music can surround the inner prayers that we long to offer.

## PRAYERS OF INTERCESSION

Until this moment, the language of the service has been general in nature. It has expressed what the

Church prays for in every time and place. Now, there is an opportunity to put into words concerns that are more immediate, and which may impinge directly on the lives of worshippers and the needs of the world.

In many cathedrals and chapels, this is where the service may end, especially on weekdays. The clergy and choir leave as organ music is played (except on Fridays).

# CONCLUSION

### HYMN

*In many places, especially at weekends and on festivals of the Christian year, a hymn is sung. This is a final act of prayer, praise or thanksgiving. Usually, the hymn will reflect the season of the year, the time of day, or resonate with what has been voiced earlier in the service.*

### BLESSING

*This concluding act is a significant moment, inviting us to take leave of the worship that has been offered. As we return to the demands and opportunities of life, we are assured that the peace and blessing of God will surround us.*

### ORGAN VOLUNTARY

This is the final element of the service (unless the service has not been accompanied by the organ, e.g. on Fridays). It affords an opportunity to give our attention to the music and enjoy it for its own sake (much as we might with a work of art – or another person).

In the pages that follow, we shall explore the various components of Choral Evensong in more detail, with suggestions as to how they can inform different levels of exploration and participation. This comes with both warning and reassurance. I have deliberately not attempted to say everything that could possibly be said about the various elements to Choral Evensong. The territory is too expansive for an introductory guide that is intended to trigger reflection, to enable the reader to inhabit an act of worship, and to feel more at home in it. Worship can take a lifetime of experience as we become familiar with its contours and discover new landmarks and gain fresh insights. We should never become anxious about understanding it completely in as short a time as possible. With God, there is always more to discover.

I have attempted to offer a degree of historical perspective, as well insights from recent scholarship, where these might enlarge an appreciation of the distinctive quality of Evensong. I have also suggested how some of the more challenging or culturally strange elements can become more familiar companions, informing the way we worship today. For those who are interested in exploring some of these issues in greater detail, I have provided suggestions for further reading at the end of the book.

# 3

# AN ACCLAMATION OF PRAISE

## *The Responses*

O Lord, open thou our lips
And our mouth shall shew forth thy praise.

O God, make speed to save us:
O Lord, make haste to help us.

Glory be to the Father, and to the Son,
and to the Holy Ghost.
As it was in the beginning, is now, and ever shall be,
world without end. Amen.

Praise ye the Lord.
The Lord's name be praised.

THESE SHORT ACCLAMATIONS sung at the beginning of Choral Evensong start with words from the psalms. They have been part of the Church's daily prayer for over 1500 years, taking us further back in history to provide a direct link to the worship of Judaism from which Christianity emerged.

The musical settings to which these words are sung

range from the simpler settings dating from the Tudor and Jacobean periods (e.g. Thomas Tallis, William Byrd, Thomas Tomkins and Richard Ayleward) to more harmonically adventurous settings from the twentieth century (e.g. Kenneth Leighton, Herbert Howells and Philip Moore).

# IN THE BEGINNING

The first couplet is from Psalm 51 (verse 17). It was originally only ever used to begin the first service of the monastic day, which took place in the dark hours before sunrise. The second is from Psalm 70 (verse 1) and was used at all subsequent services during the day. John Cassian (*c*. 360-435 CE)[8] recounts the practice of beginning prayer in this way among the monks of the Egyptian desert. In the sixth century, the Rule of St Benedict[9] specifies in detail the form of each of the monastic services and how they are to begin, and adopts the same pattern recorded by Cassian.

When Thomas Cranmer devised the orders for Morning and Evening Prayer in the first *Book of Common Prayer* of 1549, he adopted this monastic pattern and combined the two couplets with which Evensong begins. All subsequent revisions of the Prayer Book between 1552 and 1662 followed this pattern.[10]

Several commentators[11] have noted that the monastic day begins (as our worship today begins) with this appeal to God to open our lips, to be in our speech and our song, because there are moments and encounters during the average day when God is no longer on our lips. It serves to remind us that, as these words shape our speaking and thinking, we are there for God as God is there for us. It is expressed in a prayer that probably originated in France in the fifteenth century and became popular in English devotional books in the late fifteenth and early sixteenth centuries:

God be in my head, and in my understanding;
God be in mine eyes, and in my looking;
God be in my mouth, and in my speaking;
God be in my heart, and in my thinking;
God be at mine end, and at my departing.

# RECURRING GLORY

The two couplets from the psalms are followed by a short hymn of praise, beginning 'Glory be to the Father ....' This is known as a doxology (its first word in Greek being *doxa*, meaning 'glory'). Again, this has long been a part of Christian daily prayer, certainly from the last decades of the fourth century.[12] Like other elements of Evensong, it is an echo of Christianity's Jewish origins, where we find examples of doxologies throughout the Hebrew Bible (or Old Testament) as well as the Christian scriptures.

The dating of its early use in Christian worship is significant. It reflects the relatively recent way in which belief in God as Father, Son and Holy Spirit, first encountered in the New Testament letters, had begun to be agreed and expressed in the creeds – notably after the Council of Nicea in 325 CE. This short burst of praise is a means of acknowledging that, when we worship, God is the undeniable focus; and it is to God that our energy, concentration and imagination is directed. We acknowledge the multi-dimensional character of God as the Trinity of persons within one single reality.

It is a short hymn that underscores how worship is as much an expression of the faith of the Church as it is the feelings and insights of individual worshippers. It also illustrates how Christian belief is shaped through the experience of those who worship; as we pray first, before reflecting on that experiencing to discern its meaning and significance. In short, it is simply the way the Church has been saying 'this is the reality at the heart of this vast and mysterious universe' from a relatively early moment in its history. Yet the glory we give to God is reciprocal. In the accounts of creation at the beginning of the Hebrew Bible, we first discover the astonishing truth that human beings are created to reflect the glory of God and carry the divine image.

This is the first of several times that these words will be used in the course of Evensong. It is usually sung at the end of every psalm, and at the conclusion of each of the canticles. You may also hear similar words used at the conclusion of the prayers near the end of the service; and (if there is one) in the blessing with which the worship concludes.

## ALLELUIA!

This short opening section of Evensong ends with one of the visceral utterances of joy in Judaism and Christianity. 'Praise ye the Lord' is an English translation of the Hebrew phrase *Halelu'jah*, literally meaning 'Praise God.' It occurs more than twenty times in the psalms. By the time Christians worshipped publicly, there are references to its use in monastic and cathedral worship in its Greek or Latin form (Alleluia) – both at the beginning of worship (as it is at Evensong), and at other points in the services.[13] In the first *Book of Common Prayer* (1549), Cranmer initially provides the English translation, adding the Latin form (which would have been a natural part of the praying vocabulary of most people) to be used in the Easter season. After the revision of 1552, only the English form is used.[14]

It is an intensely succinct eruption of delight. It acts as a climactic full-stop that contains more than any other words can possibly express. It is as much a cry of triumph as a sigh of relief. Christians and Jews have used this phrase in many different life situations to acknowledge that God is the source of all life and the origin of goodness and compassion. It is used in times of gladness and sorrow: at a marriage as well as a funeral. It is a way of voicing our recognition that all that is good in life comes from God; and, even when we feel overwhelmed by grief, guilt or failure, God is greater than the forces and feelings that might overwhelm us. This is why, for Christians, 'Alleluia' is the great shout of rejoicing during the 50 days from Easter to Pentecost, as we celebrate the resurrection of Jesus, and the victory of life and love over darkness and death.

# WORDS FOR REFLECTION

By naming God as recipient of our praise, we are directed away from ourselves toward God, which is why doxology can be described as a… self-emptying act. In praise-giving, the 'I' or the 'we' of a people or congregation becomes other-centred, not self-centred.

Catherine LaCugna[15]

Glory be to God for dappled things –
For skies of couple-colour as a brinded cow;
For rose-moles all in stipple upon trout that swim;
Fresh-firecoal chestnut-falls; finches' wings;
Landscape plotted and pieced – fold, fallow, and plough;
And áll trádes, their gear and tackle and trim.

All things counter, original, spare, strange;
Whatever is fickle, freckled (who knows how?)
With swift, slow; sweet, sour; adazzle, dim;
He fathers-forth whose beauty is past change:
Praise him.

Gerard Manley Hopkins[16]

# LIGHTEN OUR DARKNESS

Our doxology is our recognition of the truth, the wonderful reality of our creation and salvation, and our invitation to dance with God for eternity in friendship and love. Doxology is praise: praise that changes not God but us. We awake. We recognize the beauty and goodness of the infinite God. We look into the kaleidoscope of God's marvellous works, and we are changed from despair to overwhelming hope that 'if God is for us, who is against us?' (Romans 8.31).

Nicholas Ayo[17]

Real praise is about forgetting myself, even my feelings, so that the sheer beauty and radiance of something beyond myself comes alive in me.

Rowan Williams[18]

# 4

# ALL HUMAN LIFE IS HERE

## *The Psalms*

THE PSALMS ARE a book of 150 hymns in the Hebrew Bible (or Old Testament) and have been a central feature of both Jewish and Christian worship for millennia. They were part of the worshipping experience of Jesus; and the Christian martyr of the twentieth century; Dietrich Bonhoeffer (1906-45)[19] famously described them the 'prayer book of Jesus.' He was echoing an insight that takes us back to the earliest days of Christianity's emergence from its roots in Judaism. The New Testament writers, as well as the major personalities of early Christianity, delighted in quoting from the psalms to illustrate how the teaching of Jesus, and events in his life, were being foretold.

The Psalms were composed to be sung. As well as hearing them sung at Evensong to Anglican Chant, composers have set words from the Psalms over many centuries. Many of them are sung regularly as anthems (see p. 90ff.).

The Psalms at Evensong are sung using the translation included in the *Book of Common Prayer* by Miles Coverdale (1488-1569). Coverdale's translation, which dates from the early 1550s, drew on the Latin translation of the scriptures used before the Reformation (known as the 'Vulgate' translation) and the version produced by the German

Reformer, Martin Luther (1483-1546). Because this translation has been included in all subsequent revisions of the *Book of Common Prayer*, it has become widely known and loved throughout the Anglican world. It is not the most accurate translation; but it has a rhythmic, almost musical quality.

# THE VOICE OF LONG EXPERIENCE

In the *Book of Common Prayer* the Psalms are described as 'The Psalms of David.' This reflects the underlying view in earlier centuries that they were the outcome of a single authorship, ascribed to the Jewish king, David, whose life is chronicled in the Hebrew Bible.[20] Scholarly consensus over recent centuries has concluded that their composition took place over a long period of time, possibly extending five centuries; and that they were probably edited and collated into a single collection during the time of the Second Temple in Jerusalem (early fifth century BCE).[21] Collectively, the Psalms are often called the Psalter.

The lengthy period over which the Psalter evolved reflects the highs and lows of Jewish history and of human experience. It also reflects the worshipping practice of the Jews: sometimes describing their rituals; at other times articulating their beliefs. The prevailing outlook of the Psalter is that the world is created and held by God. This, in turn, invites humanity's praise and prayer, because God's bearing towards the human race can be recognized in the events of history as well as the experience of individuals. Sometimes God acts in response to humanity's prayer; at other times he appears not to do so (often expressed by the metaphor of God hiding his face). All of this is expressed in many different ways and the Psalter encompasses the contrasting experience of praise and lament, hope and despair, tragedy and triumph, exile and home-coming, grief and delight. It also recounts some of the decisive narratives of Jewish history and the ways God acts through them.

## ORIGINS AND PURPOSES

There are many ways of categorizing the different psalms within the Psalter. One approach, that reflects a widespread consensus over the past century and more, was pioneered by the German scholar, Hermann Gunkel (1862-1932).[22] His concern was with the historical, religious and social setting of the Bible, and this led him to place the Psalms in the following broad categories:

- **Hymns** that celebrate God's glory and sovereignty over creation, God's choice of Jerusalem, and the assurance that God's justice will prevail when the innocent suffer. Others are in form of personal thanksgiving. Some clearly arise from the worship of the Temple, as well as journeys made by pilgrims to Jerusalem (e.g. psalms 8, 23, 33, 47, 48, 65, 66, 68, 78, 82, 84, 103, 104, 105-107, 120-134, 136, 130, 145-150).

- **Laments** that express both national and individual despair, often in the face of a particular disaster or misfortune, and the suffering is often described with striking honesty. Sometimes, a lament may call on God to deal with those who are deemed to be responsible for the ordeal being borne; or a plea of innocence by those who suffer. Many end on a note of praise and thanksgiving, as those who have experienced injustice renew their trust in the salvation and deliverance that comes from God alone (e.g. psalms 3, 6, 12, 22, 42-44, 60-62, 73, 74, 79, 90, 137, 142, 143). In some cathedrals and chapels, certain verses from the psalms of lament (and the whole of Psalm 58) are not sung, as they express intentions of violence towards others that are considered inconsistent with Christian teaching. In other places, these verses are retained, because they are considered to provide an opportunity to state honestly what many people really feel and experience when they have been wronged. Only by naming what we are experiencing in life's darkest moments can we begin to address the motives and intentions that can be considered afresh in the light of God's mercy and love.

- **Royal Psalms** that are focussed either on God's sovereignty over creation and human affairs, on the king who rules in God's name, or on aspects of royal character (e.g. psalms 2, 21, 24, 45, 47, 89, 93, 99, 110, 144).

In addition to these broad categories, there are psalms that praise the law of God as an expression of his wisdom and faithfulness (e.g. psalms 19, 111 and 119) as well as those psalms that express the virtues of personal faithfulness and integrity, especially in the face of suffering (e.g. psalms 1, 86 and 91).

## CHOICE AND CHANGE

In the monastic tradition, the psalms were divided up to be sung at the various services that punctuated the day so that the whole Psalter was sung over the course of a week. With the publication of the first *Book of Common Prayer*, Thomas Cranmer kept to the principal of this pattern, but adapted it into a form considered more digestible for clergy and people to use together twice each day. He adapted the monastic pattern by devising a scheme for the Psalter to be said or sung over the course of a month. Today, many cathedrals and chapels follow this pattern (except, perhaps, on Sundays), while others follow more recent schemes, where the psalms are chosen either to relate to the biblical readings in the service, or to reflect the season of the year. This more recent approach does, in fact, reflect the more ancient practice of daily prayer in non-monastic urban settings, where psalms were chosen to reflect the time of day or the season of the year, and where only selected psalms were ever sung and never the entire Psalter.[23]

## SYMMETRICAL POETRY

One of the constant features we encounter in the psalms is a literary pattern known as 'parallelism.' This is where an idea, intention or belief is expressed in one line of a verse; and then, effectively, repeated by using different words. For example,

> Ponder my words, O Lord:
> consider my meditation.

(Psalm 5:1)

or

> The Lord hath heard my petition:
> the Lord will receive my prayer.

(Psalm 6:9)

Some forms of parallelism emphasise contrasting ideas within a verse. For example,

> But the Lord knoweth the way of the righteous:
> and the way of the ungodly shall perish.

(Psalm 6:7)

or

> The lions do lack, and suffer hunger:
> but they who seek the Lord shall want
> no manner of thing that is good.

(Psalm 34:10)

Other forms of parallelism express an idea in one line of the verse, and then develop it by suggesting a possible outcome. For example,

> Surely thy loving-kindness and mercy shall follow me
> all the days of my life :
> and I will dwell in the house of the Lord for ever.

(Psalm 23:6)

> For thou art my strong rock, and my castle:
> be thou also my guide, and lead me for thy name's sake.

(Psalm 31:4)

These and other forms of parallelism are a distinctive feature in Hebrew poetry. They can be helpful in enabling the words and ideas in the psalms to become lodged in the memory and take root in our consciousness – as well as our praying – over a period of time. We simply need to create the space for the words, heard many times, to make themselves at home in our hearing and reflection. This parallelism is also expressed in the way the psalms are sung at Evensong: as one half of the verse is sung by one side of the choir, with the other being taken up by the opposite side.

Coverdale's translation with its rhythmic patterns and the repetitive shape of the Anglican chant to which it is usually sung, allows the words and music to merge in a way that they become, literally, memorable. It is often said that if you quote the verse of a psalm from Coverdale's translation of the Psalms to someone who has been singing them for many years, such as a chorister in a cathedral choir, they can usually respond instinctively with the verse that follows it!

## MUSIC AND MEDITATION

Biblical scholarship has been helpful in enabling us to recognise the different types of psalm and the life-setting from which they emerged. Equally important is how countless generations of Christians (and Jews) have prayed these words over the course of many centuries, finding that they are an authentic expression of the range of experiences and emotions that punctuate our lives.

The parallelism in the poetry of the psalms has been emphasised in the Jewish practice of singing them. A slight pause is observed half-way through the verse to allow one idea to be voiced, and then to be repeated or expanded in the next. This is a tradition that continued (and still continues) in Christian worship. In monastic worship, where the psalms are sung to plainsong, a pause is naturally observed after the first half of the verse. You may hear that tradition being continued in cathedrals and chapels, today, particularly on those days when the service is being sung by the adult voices alone, when the psalms are most often sung to plainsong.

Whether the psalms are sung to plainsong or Anglican chant (which is, essentially, a harmonised development of plainsong),[24] their musical treatment can allow us space to approach them in a way that complements the insights of biblical scholarship. It is a way that has shaped monastic communities for centuries. It is simply to allow the psalms – whether an entire psalm or a verse (or half-verse) – to speak directly to us in the moment of hearing it; and then allow it to feed our thinking and praying. Particular words or phrases from of the psalms, along with the music to which they are set, can lodge in our thoughts and memories (often without us deliberately setting out to find them). That one word or phrase can trigger our praying over a period of time. It requires no scholarly insight or technical grasp of the theology underpinning the words. It also frees us from the constraint of having to follow every word of every psalm. Instead, we are encouraged to simply listen, and to be open to receiving an unexpected gift. As we listen to the singing of the psalms, we can relax into their rhythm: not so much to understand the words in terms of analysing them meticulously; but simply to be attentive to what they might offer us in that moment.

## SHAPING LIFE AND FAITH

This is an approach that is not far removed from the insights arising from a strand of more recent biblical scholarship, typified by the American Protestant scholar, Walter Brueggemann (b.1933).[25]

In (what he calls) a Rhetorical approach to their interpretation, he suggests that the Psalms can be approached as a body of poetic wisdom, encouraging us to discover how they can inform and shape the life of faith and our response to the world. They are an expression of how 'the community of faith has heard and continues to hear the sovereign speech of God ... in its depths of need and in its heights of celebration' and reflect 'the voice of our own common humanity, gathered over a long period of time'.[26]

As an example, Psalms 73 and 74, which may be sung on the fourteenth evening of each month, speak into situations of disorientation by naming the grief and injustice that is all-too-real in the world we know. We may find some of the vengeful sentiments expressed in them difficult; but they are an authentic expression of the pain of a people engaging with God in world-shattering circumstances, when they even begin to doubt the faithfulness of their Creator. Nonetheless, for Brueggemann, the Psalter needs to be viewed as a whole, where psalms of *dis*orientation are resolved by psalms of *re*-orientation, when the praise of God is foremost, enabling us to see the world differently and God as the one whose love and justice triumphs over evil and tragedy. This is one of the insights that the Psalter offers, as it encourages us to see how worship can change the way we see life.

However we approach the Psalms, their placing in the contours of choral worship can encourage a deeper sense of receptivity as we worship. It can free us from the need to constantly predetermine what the outcome might be. It removes the need to be anxious or disengaged if the mood and sentiment of the psalms do not directly reflect our lived experience on a particular day. In all probability, they will on another day. Crucially, by encountering the psalms in this way, we are simply given the freedom to receive whatever may emerge from them, to be encouraged, challenged or consoled that, for this specific moment, 'this is the word of the Lord.'

## ENDING IN PRAISE

Each of the psalms ends with the same doxology that is sung at the beginning of the service (Glory be to the Father, and to the Son; and to the Holy Ghost ...). This is a practice that first appeared at a relatively early point of Christian history, and was known among the monastic communities of the desert before becoming a widespread practice by the sixth century.

This Christian practice is also a reflection of the doxologies that exist in the Hebrew text of the Psalms. The Psalms are divided into five sections (or books) and each ends with a Jewish form of doxology (the divisions come after psalms 41, 72, 89, 106 and 150). This is, in part, a reflection of the five-fold shape of the *Torah* (the Jewish Law contained in the first five books of the Hebrew Bible, Genesis, Exodus, Leviticus, Numbers and Deuteronomy).

Doxology is a particularly Jewish form expression in worship which Christians have adopted and developed. As the psalms voice the breadth and depth of human experience, the last word is always an acclamation in praise of God. At the darkest moments of life, as well as in times of delight and thankfulness, the instinct is always to acknowledge the constancy and mercy of God, who is the origin of all life, the sustainer of the world, who has promised to be with us to end of time.

# WORDS FOR REFLECTION

Thanks, ten thousand times I thank him,
Thank him while I've breath and tongue
For being what he is, to worship
And for ever be the theme of song!

Ann Griffiths[27]

The music varied hugely, from sparse polyphonic and plainchant settings used on nights when only mens' voices were available through lush Victorian settings and turn of the century tearjerkers to challenging contemporary ones … After several exposures, Laura found she was enjoying the psalms, with their frequent bouts of despair or indignation, and the unexpected charm of the readings … The words, especially those of the nunc dimittis and the repeated references to night and stillness ... the inevitable identification of the end of the day with the end of life, tended to bring on a curious fit of nostalgia or species of homesickness… that could make her tearful if she didn't guard against it.

Patrick Gale[28]

# ALL HUMAN LIFE IS HERE

I wake and feel the fell of dark, not day.
What hours, O what black hours we have spent
This night! what sights you, heart, saw; ways you went!
And more must, in yet longer light's delay.
 With witness I speak this. But where I say
Hours I mean years, mean life. And my lament
Is cries countless, cries like dead letters sent
To dearest him that lives alas! away.

Gerard Manley Hopkins[29]

If the psalm prays, you pray.
If the psalm laments, you lament.
If the psalm exalts, you rejoice.
If it hopes, you hope.
If it fears, you fear.
Everything written here is a mirror for us.

Augustine of Hippo[30]

God is wholly in every place ... We may imagine God to be as
the air and the sea, and we all enclosed in his circle, wrapped
up in the lap of his infinite nature, or as infants in the wombs
of their pregnant mothers; and we can no more be removed
from the presence of God than from our own being.

Jeremy Tayor[31]

# 5

# A WORD ONCE SPOKEN

*The Readings*

THE SINGING OF the psalms is followed by two readings (sometimes called Lessons) from other parts of the Bible. Like many other elements of our worship, this is a feature that we have inherited from our Jewish roots, where the singing of psalms and a reading from the *Torah* (or Law), contained in the first five books of the Hebrew Bible (what Christians call the Old Testament) provided the basic structure of worship in the synagogue (as it still does today). In that sense, all Christian worship affords a central place to the Bible.

As a collection of diverse texts that Christians hold sacred, the Bible is the record of God's dealing with humanity, written by different people, in different literary styles, for different religious communities, and at different times in history. It is one of the ways by which the community of faith hands on, from generation to generation, the memories, beliefs and insights of God's involvement in the world, the life of his people, and in the death and resurrection of Jesus Christ.

The Hebrew Bible (the Old Testament), is sacred for Jews as well as Christians. It contains the Jewish Law, along with historical narratives, the oracles of the prophets, and different forms of wisdom and poetry. The New Testament contains the four Gospels that record the known and remembered words and actions of Jesus, as well as the writings of his early followers that reflect on the significance of his life, death and resurrection. The Hebrew Bible and the New Testament together are regarded as 'Scripture' by Christians. This expresses the belief that it is a collection of texts that records and articulates the word of God, once spoken in a particular situation and to particular people, and that it continues to embody the truth of God's bearing towards the world and the human race. This is why, in some acts of worship (for example at the Eucharist), readings from the Bible conclude with the words 'This is the word of the Lord.'

## INTELLIGENCE AND INSIGHT

The history of how the Christian Church has understood the Bible as the word of God is a complex and fascinating story – just like the Bible itself. It can only be touched upon superficially in an introductory guide such as this. Nonetheless, it is important to appreciate that, even from early periods of Christian history, as well as from the second half of the seventeenth century in Europe and America, the Bible has been the subject of critical and interpretative enquiry. This has been pioneered as much by people of faith, including significant personalities in the history of the Church, as it has by those who have adopted a more sceptical stance.

As a scholarly movement, this has largely been driven by a concern for truth, to engage in fruitful and constructive encounter with the texts of the Bible (including their literary variety, their original life setting, as well as their meaning for the people who first heard them); and to allow them to speak on their own terms today. Put simply, biblical scholarship arises from an overarching concern to treat the Bible with seriousness and respect. Only by interrogating the Bible with intelligence and insight can its meaning as the word of the Lord, once spoken to our forebears in the faith, be a source of wisdom and divine revelation today and in the future.

## PUBLIC READING

Both the urban (or cathedral) and the monastic practices of the early Christian centuries placed considerable emphasis on the public reading of Scripture. The Benedictine tradition (which governed the life of many English cathedrals before the sixteenth-century Reformation – and influenced others that were not Benedictine or monastic foundations) envisions a community centred round the reading of Scripture: not only at times of worship; but also at mealtimes and at meetings to discuss the everyday business of the community. *The Rule of St Benedict* is punctuated by multiple references to Scripture as the foundation for ordering the community's life; and is insistent that it is never enough to hear, to read, or even to love the Scriptures. They also inform the words and actions of all in the community.[32]

## REFORMED READING OF THE BIBLE

The publication of the first *Book of Common Prayer* (*BCP*) in 1549 was the outcome of a decades-long period during which there had been a growing co-operation and collaboration across Europe to make not only the texts of the Bible more widely available and more easily understood; but also to democratise learning and intellectual enquiry generally. It was a seismic shift in the history of the West. The dissolution of the monasteries, coupled to the invention of printing, meant that the Bible was no longer a text to be regulated by religious professionals alone. The desire that worship, conducted entirely in Latin for at least the previous 600 years, should now be in 'a language understanded of the people' (as it is expressed in the Preface to the *BCP*) meant that the reading and interpretation of Scripture became more accessible. English Reformers, such as Thomas Cranmer, did not act in isolation from their counterparts on the European mainland; and it is evident that the Church of England's framework of belief (its doctrine), not least its understanding of the Bible, was shaped as much by the cross-cultivation of ideas between London, Geneva, Strasbourg and Zurich, as it was by the distinctive circumstances in which the Reformation evolved in England, Wales and Ireland.[33]

When he adapted the monastic pattern of worship for clergy and people to use together, Thomas Cranmer retained the Benedictine principle of the public reading of the Bible. Given that the Reformation was, in no small part, a reclaiming of the scriptural foundations for the Church, its doctrine and its worship, this is hardly surprising. Nonetheless, there was to be more of it in each service than there had been in the monastic services. A chapter from the Hebrew scriptures and a chapter from the New Testament would be read at each of the two daily services of Morning and Evening Prayer. The New Testament would be heard three times over the course of a year; and the Old Testament over a span of one year. This is a pattern that was largely observed well into the second half of the nineteenth century when more flexible approaches to aspects of the Church of England's worship began to emerge.

# READING THE BIBLE IN THE CHURCH OF ENGLAND

One of the great principles of the Reformation was *Sola Scriptura* (by Scripture alone), and this is foundational for many churches that owe their origins to this period of history, and which describe themselves as Protestant or Reformed. As it evolved during the late sixteenth and early seventeenth centuries, the Church of England adopted the different and distinctive approach of *Prima Scriptura* (Scripture first) where the Bible was to be understood and interpreted in the light of tradition and reason.[34] Unlike some other European Protestant churches, the Church of England evolved by embracing a *via media* (or middle way) between the radical Puritans of the sixteenth century and the historic claims of the Catholic Church. Put simply, the insights of human reason (including scientific discovery, as well as the arts and humanities) offer a valid perspective to make sense of the Bible in our own time, alongside insights from Christianity's historical experience, such as Councils of the Church, the work of Christian saints and scholars, and the insights of preaching and teaching in the early Christian centuries. This is one reason why the Church of England has been open to the influence of developing strands of biblical scholarship. Its scholars (including some of its bishops) have often been at the forefront of the European movement of scrutinising the Bible that began in the late-eighteenth century and continues to the present day.

This provides a framework for hearing and interpreting the scriptures that is much larger than any one individual's understanding of the biblical text – or that of any specific culture or period of history. We hear them, and interpret them, through a dynamic tradition of worship, insight and experience that is shared by the whole Church. In that sense, the Bible is not a closed book, any more than it is any one individual's personal possession. Historically, the Church of England has never treated the Bible in the same way that Muslims might regard the *Qu'ran*, for example. Christian revelation is not conclusively confined between the covers of a book (or collection of books): it is primarily seen in the life, death and resurrection of Jesus Christ, to which the Bible bears witness. In that sense, it is always open to new discoveries and new truth the more we hear it and reflect on it. As one contemporary scholar has put it, the question is not so much *is* this the word of the Lord, as *how is* this the word of the Lord?[35]

The creative momentum around Scripture speaking from the past into the present, its impact on the sweep of Christian history and experience, and the possibility of fresh insights, is expressed in some lines from a hymn by a twentieth-century biblical scholar:

Not far beyond the sea, nor high
above the heavens, but very nigh
your voice, O God, is heard.
For each new step of faith we take
you have more truth and light to break
forth from your holy word.

Rooted and grounded in your love,
with saints on earth and saints above
we join in full accord:
to know the breadth, length, depth and height,
the crucified and risen might
of Christ, the incarnate Word.[36]

# CHALLENGING SELF-SELECTION

One of the questions that can puzzle people is the issue of how passages from the Bible are chosen to be read at Evensong. This is especially the case when you may attend occasionally and find yourself 'dropping in' at the mid-way point of a narrative that involves inexplicable violence, or a passage that is culturally strange and challenging, or even one that strikes you as offensive. Certainly, you may hear a passage from the Bible that leaves you wondering what came before it – and how it will end after it seems to conclude in mid-flow.

This is a reflection of the pattern of reading Scripture that evolved in monastic communities, where the community was stable and the same people gathered every day at every service. This ensured that, as the whole Bible was being heard, it was heard in *context* and not as isolated fragments. In certain respects, this is a continuation of a practice Christianity absorbed from its Jewish roots, where a *parasha* or section of the *Torah* has been read at worship in the synagogue on the Sabbath over a 54 week cycle since the period of exile in the sixth century BCE.[37]

Similarly, Cranmer (and those who followed him in revising subsequent editions of the *BCP*) worked on the assumption that clergy and people praying together twice every day would hear readings from the Bible in succession (what is known as *lectio continua*). They were also responding to an emerging tendency at the time, especially among some radical Puritan groups, to randomly select detached passages of Scripture to advocate and endorse what were regarded as contentious theological claims.

The scheme for reading the Bible is known as a Lectionary (derived from the Latin word *Lectio* 'to read'). By adopting this monastic (and Jewish) principal of devising an ordered plan for reading the scriptures, Cranmer and his fellow reformers were accentuating the importance of engaging with the Bible as part of *common* prayer: as something the Church does together as one body. To emphasise this, Cranmer's scheme for reading the Bible at Morning and Evening Prayer was based on the work of other European reformers as well as the reforming Spanish Roman Catholic, Francisco de Quiñones (1482-1540).

## IN COMPANY WITH OTHERS

Although we live in a different theological and cultural climate, the Church of England has continued to use a lectionary for its principal acts of worship. Today (especially in relation to the readings at the Eucharist) this is a scheme broadly shared with many other Christian churches throughout the world. Few cathedrals, chapels and churches, today, will use Cranmer's original 'one chapter per reading' lectionary. Most will use a form of the most recent lectionary that accompanied the publication of *Common Worship* beginning in 2000. For most of the year, this provides readings that are heard successively from day to day, though on Sundays and major festivals the readings will be twinned in a thematic way and not be part of the daily continuous cycle. For much of the year, it selects passages from the books of the Bible that reflect the progressing seasons of the Christian year. For example, during Advent, with its emphasis on Christ's coming in glory and the end times, the Hebrew prophets (notably Isaiah), with their tone of longing for salvation, are coupled to readings from Revelation and the letters to the Thessalonians in the New Testament, that accentuate the need to be watchful as Christ has promised to return to his waiting people.

It is also widely recognised that many people attending Choral Evensong in cathedrals and other churches will not attend each and every day, or even regularly. With this in mind, an alternative lectionary has been devised more recently (called a 'pillar' lectionary because it provides stand-alone readings in pairs). It enables passages from the Bible to be heard comprehensibly without the necessity of having to hear what was read the previous (or following) day.

# HEARING AND RESPONDING:
# A RECIPROCAL CONVERSATION

The discussion about the how the Bible is read as part of the flow of Choral Evensong, and how parts of it are chosen to be read, brings us back to a crucial question. How can the Bible be a source of truth and wisdom in a world that is very different from the eras in which the texts of the scriptures first emerged? What is the most fruitful way of engaging with the Bible's capacity to inspire, affirm, comfort, challenge, and even rebuke, today?

Unquestionably, the insights of biblical scholarship are helpful – not least in enabling worshippers to develop a discriminating sense of hearing different styles of biblical literature. The Bible does not 'speak' on a flat, one-dimensional level. Poetry communicates its meaning differently to historical narrative, for example, and prophecy is a different medium to that of the Gospels. Nonetheless, having a sense of a particular reading's context, or the characteristics of its literary style, is just one part of engaging with Scripture. At Evensong, we are primarily engaged in worship, and this carries an implicit invitation simply to receive what is offered, to reflect upon it with insight, and to discover how the readings from the Bible can be a means of encountering the word and will of God for us today. As the English Baptist scholar, Neville Clark, memorably suggested:

> Scripture exists for the sake of proclamation . . . It is a Word once spoken that clamours to be spoken again, a story once told that presses towards retelling . . . it is restlessly pushing back towards the patterns of oral speech, address and conversation, intent on recreating the immediacy of face-to-face encounter.[38]

The monastic tradition of hearing the scriptures in worship is one fruitful way of hearing the Bible at Evensong, particularly as the *BCP* emerged from this centuries-long momentum. It regards the Bible not primarily as a set of instructions, but as a source of wisdom. It encourages us to listen to Scripture as a gift, with an openness to what we might receive, perhaps out of the blue, without the relentless pressure either to expect an outcome every time we hear it, or to control the meaning of the text. It also frees us from the constraints and pressures of time. The monastic pattern is fully open to the possibility that the word of the Lord may be received from hearing Scripture, quite unpredictably, at a later time when absorbed in an entirely different activity. As a word or a phrase may lodge in the memory and consciousness, it is perfectly possible to experience something like a delayed reaction, even months later.[39]

## AN ENERGETIC PULSE

Understood in this way, hearing the Bible as part of the shape and flow of Evensong, invites us to develop our capacity to listen – and to listen actively as a vital dimension of our engagement with Scripture. Listening in this way is not simply passive reception, but equips us for a dynamic dialogue with what Scripture offers us. Scripture read in worship is part of an on-going conversation, where carefully developed attentiveness to another voice leads to a fitting response, if the dialogue to carry on or be resumed later. As with any conversation, there will be elements of questioning, agreement, empathy, and even disagreement, as well as the triggering of new ideas and insights in our response. This is another way of signifying that the Bible is not fixed or static, but more like a pulse of energy that beats through the life and worship of the Church, continually inviting our attentiveness and evoking our response. Ultimately, our focus in worship is never the text of Scripture as an end in itself; but the living God to whom it directs our hearts and minds and wills.

## SPEAKING THE LOCAL LANGUAGE

On Sundays, especially in college chapels, one additional feature of Evensong that both amplifies the readings from Scripture and addresses issues of current interest and concern is a sermon. This is an opportunity to explore how the ancient text of can be the starting point for the Church to have an ongoing dialogue with many areas of contemporary life, such as science and technology, the arts, politics, education and the media, as well as a raft of pressing cultural questions and concerns. Very often, the sermons at Evensong may be a themed series during the course of an academic term, delivered by those with a specialist interest in the topic under consideration. Some of them may be ordained clergy; others will be poets, musicians, journalists, political and cultural figures, academics and even figures from the world of sport.

Delivering a sermon at Evensong can be a delicate balancing act: partly because one of the attractions of Choral Evensong (especially on weekdays) is precisely the fact that there is no sermon; and because a period of extended speech can often feel out of place in a service that has more of a contemplative – rather than instructive – character. Nonetheless, if approached with a degree of pastoral insight and theological imagination, using no more words than are actually necessary, a sermon at Evensong can be an effective way of inviting worshippers to cultivate a God-centred view of the world they inhabit, with all its stresses and opportunities. The best sermons will always be as carefully crafted as the prayer, poetry, architecture and music that characterizes the rest of Evensong. It will never try to say everything; but allow worshippers space to draw their own inferences and conclusions, rather than seek to control how we should think. It should be encouraging and energizing – and never leave anyone feeling inadequate, got at, or excluded.

At its best, a sermon at Choral Evensong can be another means of enabling us to engage effectively with Scripture (and the Christian tradition more broadly) with intelligence and discernment, nourishing our search for God, as well as inspiring us to live more hopefully and generously.

# WORDS FOR REFLECTION

The ministry of the word ... is like a looking-glass ... We behold the image of God as it is presented before us in the word, in the sacraments, and, in fine, in the whole of the service of the Church.

John Calvin[40]

Consecutive reading of biblical books forces everyone who wants to hear to put himself, or to allow himself to be found, where God has acted once and for all for the salvation of men. We become a part of what once took place for our salvation. Forgetting and losing ourselves, we, too, pass through the Red Sea, through the desert, across the Jordan into the promised land. With Israel we fall into doubt and unbelief and through punishment and repentance experience again God's help and faithfulness. All this is not mere reverie but holy, godly reality. We are torn out of our own existence and set down in the midst of the holy history of God on earth. There God dealt with us, and there he still deals with us, our needs and our sins, in judgment and grace. It is not that God is the spectator and sharer of our present life, howsoever important that is; but rather that we are the reverent listeners and participants in God's action in the sacred story, the history of the Christ on earth.

Dietrich Bonhoeffer[41]

Oh that I knew how all thy lights combine,
And the configurations of their glorie!
Seeing not onely how each verse doth shine,
But all the constellations of the storie.

This verse marks that, and both do make a motion
Unto a third, that ten leaves off doth lie:
Then as dispersed herbs do watch a potion,
These three make up some Christians destinie:

Such are thy secrets, which my life makes good,
And comments on thee: for in ev'ry thing
Thy words do finde me out, & parallels bring,
And in another make me understood.

Starres are poore books, & oftentimes do misse:
This book of starres lights to eternall blisse.

George Herbert[42]

The Christian gospel has always sought to reconnect us with the everyday, the material, the ordinary, the local … God has spoken to us in the language we most readily understand; he has stood alongside us and has learned human speech. He has won our trust by sharing our world. He can even speak the language of fear and inner anguish and desolation, as he does on the cross, and we can think, yes, he knows us, he knows what is in us … Reading the Bible is not reading a book that's extraordinary because it is so well-written or so inspiring; it's reading ordinary words, sometimes words that pile up on each other with excitement or the sense of immense mystery, that God has taken up to tell us who he is and who we are.

Rowan Williams[43]

# 6

# REVOLUTION AND RETIREMENT

## *The Canticles*

My soul doth magnify the Lord.
And my spirit hath rejoiced in God my Saviour.
For he hath regarded : the lowliness of his handmaiden.
For behold, from henceforth : all generations shall call me
      blessed.
For he that is mighty hath magnified me: and holy is his Name.
And his mercy is on them that fear him: throughout all
      generations.
He hath shewed strength with his arm:
he hath scattered the proud in the imagination of their hearts.
He hath put down the mighty from their seat:
and hath exalted the humble and meek.
He hath filled the hungry with good things:
and the rich he hath sent empty away.
He remembering his mercy hath holpen his servant Israel :
As he promised to our forefathers, Abraham and his seed
      for ever.
Glory be to the Father, and to the Son: and to the Holy
      Ghost;
As it was in the beginning, is now, and ever shall be:
      world without end. Amen.

Lord, now lettest thou thy servant depart in peace:
according to thy word.
For mine eyes have seen thy salvation: which thou hast
prepared before the face of all people;
To be a light to lighten the Gentiles: and to be the glory
of thy people Israel.
Glory be to the Father, and to the Son: and to the Holy
Ghost;
As it was in the beginning, is now, and ever shall be:
world without end. Amen.

After each of the readings at Choral Evensong, two canticles are sung by the choir (from the Latin *canticum* meaning 'song'). The texts of both canticles are found in the New Testament, in the opening chapters of the Gospel according to Luke. They not only provide a response to the readings that precede them; but the first of the canticles also acts as a bridge between the reading from the Hebrew Bible and the reading from the New Testament. It enables us to travel from the Jewish territory of the first reading into the narratives, beliefs and hopes of the early Christian world voiced in the second reading.

The first of the two canticles, is commonly known as the *Magnificat* (the first word of its Latin text *Magnificat anima mea Dominum*). It is also described as 'the song of the Blessed Virgin Mary' in the *Book of Common Prayer*. It has been part of the Church's daily prayer from an early stage in Christian history, and has been part of Evening Prayer in the West since the sixth century CE.[44]

# JEWISH AND CHRISTIAN

The *Magnificat* appears at an early stage of the narrative of Luke's Gospel, before the birth of Christ. Mary, expecting her child Jesus, encounters her cousin, Elizabeth. She is also pregnant and expecting to give birth to John the Baptist (Luke 1:39-56). This song, which the Church has traditionally attributed to Mary (although some Greek texts of the New Testament are less clear about whether it is Mary or Elizabeth who sings it), celebrates the beginning of a new era inaugurated by God. Its origin in the Gospel makes it unquestionably a Christian song of praise. Nonetheless, like many aspects of the gospels, it strongly echoes Christianity's Jewish roots: in particular, the song Hannah proclaimed at the birth of the prophet Samuel (1 Samuel 2:1-10); and the psalms (notably Psalm 113):

> My heart rejoiceth in the Lord, mine horn is exalted in the
> Lord: my mouth is enlarged over
> > mine enemies;
> because I rejoice in thy salvation …
> Talk no more so exceeding proudly;
> let not arrogancy come out of your mouth:
> for the Lord is a God of knowledge,
> and by him actions are weighed …
> The Lord maketh poor, and maketh rich:
> he bringeth low, and lifteth up.
> He raiseth up the poor out of the dust,
> and lifteth up the beggar from the dunghill,
> to set them among princes,
> and to make them inherit the throne of glory …
> He will keep the feet of his saints,
> and the wicked shall be silent in darkness …

Praise the Lord, ye servants : O praise the Name of the Lord ...
Who is like unto the Lord our God, that hath his dwelling so
high: and yet humbleth himself to behold the things that are
in heaven and earth?
He taketh up the simple out of the dust:
and lifteth the poor out of the mire ...

The words of the *Magnificat* resonate with a persistent
theme in the Hebrew Bible: of God choosing the powerless
and poor to make known his will and purpose for the
human race. Just as the Hebrew peoples, with their history
of slavery, defeat and exile, were the ones through whom
God's glory would be revealed; the *Magnificat* and its Jewish
antecedents express the conviction that the poor, the hungry
and those without power and influence are favoured over
the strong, the wealthy and those with high social status.

## A SONG OF SUBVERSION

The fact that the *Magnificat* and the song of Hannah are
texts attributed to women in the scriptures is significant. In
the ancient Jewish and Classical cultures from which these
texts emerged, women were excluded from the arenas of
political, religious, intellectual and artistic influence, and
were afforded few social dignities or legal rights. In many
respects, they were non-persons. Consequently, this is a song
of change and transformation that celebrates hidden people
and silenced voices taking centre-stage as the visionaries
of a new world order, signifying how God's desire is often
deeply subversive of human power structures.

In this way, the *Magnificat* is a song that begins in the
Jewish world and looks forward to what will unfold in
the Gospel: of those excluded and diminished by gender,
disability, or their lack of conformity to the Jewish law,
having their dignity, as well as their place in the community,

restored. This is a theme taken up elsewhere in the New Testament, where Paul writes about the crucified Christ as a demonstration of God's power being revealed in weakness, and God favouring those whom the world regards as foolish and despised. This is a song that celebrates the incarnation, the belief that, in Jesus Christ, God is decisively involved in the pressures and constraints of life. As Evensong usually takes place in an environment of beauty and peace, the *Magnificat* focuses our attention on the wider world. The stunning architecture and the sublime music invite us to recognise that worship is never an escape from the pressures and possibilities of the everyday world. It is an opportunity to step aside for a brief moment, to be nourished by a vision of beauty and glory, where we can weigh up the agonies (as well as the possibilities) of life with greater clarity and compassion.

## YOUNG AND OLD

After the second reading, the choir sings another song from Luke's Gospel, the *Nunc Dimittis* (the first two words of its Latin translation *Nunc dimittis servam tuam, Dominum*). In contrast to the Magnificat, Luke puts these words into the mouth of an old man, Simeon. Jesus is brought to the Temple in accordance with the Jewish law, forty days after his birth. Simeon had waited a lifetime to see the promised Messiah (Luke 2:22-38). Just before death and after gazing on the face of God revealed in a tiny child, he utters this song of relieved thanksgiving. In its original setting in the Gospel, Luke places this song against the backdrop of an encounter by two people at vulnerable moments of their lives: one in advanced old age; the other in early infancy. It is a prayer of both leave-taking and looking forward to an unknown but promised future. Simeon glimpses the long-awaited hopes of the Jewish people being fulfilled in the child who is born to suffer and die for the salvation of the whole world.

This canticle has been sung at the final service of the monastic day since the fourth century.[45] Its valedictory emphasis, along with its reference to Christ as the light to lighten the gentiles, makes it appropriate for an act of worship that inaugurates sleep as darkness falls. When Thomas Cranmer combined elements of the final two services of the monastic day in the first *BCP*, he took the *Magnificat* from Evening Prayer (or Vespers) and the *Nunc Dimittis* from Night Prayer (or Compline), to frame the reading of the scriptures at Evensong.

Although it is a song that articulates a peaceful ending, the *Nunc Dimittis* is no less subversive than the *Magnificat*. It depicts the very old, Simeon and the prophet Anna who waited with him, as tellers of hope at a dark time in the history of the Jewish people. That may seem profoundly counter-cultural in a society that not only tends to disregard the insights of the old, but has an inclination to assume that, once a certain age has been reached in life, all hope of a better future is long past. It shows how the old are willing to surrender their accumulated cultural and religious baggage, and hand it on to others whose future they cannot control. They demonstrate that the salvation they have glimpsed in this child is not simply for them and people like them; but for countless millions yet to be born, and from places far beyond the horizon of their known world. This is a vision of God's desire being far greater than we can formulate or imagine.

# MUSICAL SETTINGS

Together, the musical setting of the two canticles forms a centrepiece to Choral Evensong. They are usually identified by the surname of the composer and the musical key in which they are written (e.g. Jackson in G, Stanford in B flat or Walmisley in D minor etc.). Earlier settings, dating from a period before modern musical key structures were defined, were numbered in the order in which they were composed (e.g. 'The First Service'). Some refer to the style of music (e.g. a 'Short Service' by a Tudor or Jacobean composer is usually a simple setting without much musical elaboration, and most likely to be heard on Fridays, or during Advent and Lent). Some composers since the second half of the twentieth century have often given the name of the place for which their musical setting was composed (e.g. *Collegium Regale* for King's College, Cambridge by Herbert Howells, John Tavener and Charles Wood; *Collegium Magdalenae* for Magdalen College, Oxford by Kenneth Leighton; or the Wells Service by Malcolm Archer, etc.).

Composers have approached the texts differently in composing music to the words. Some have adopted a gentle, lyrical approach (e.g. Stanford in G, Sumsion in G, Watson in E, along with some of the Tudor and Jacobean settings such as the Second Services of William Byrd and Orlando Gibbons) to reflect the feminine and elderly association of their biblical origins. Some, from various periods, are more declamatory and angular in their interpretation, to emphasise the challenge inherent in their meaning (e.g. Michael Tippett's *Collegium Sancti Johannes* for St John's College, Cambridge, Purcell in G minor, Stanford in A, the setting for Jesus College, Cambridge by William Mathias, and the *Magnificat* by Giles Swayne informed by primitive African chants). Others bestow the words with a transcendent, even mystical character (such as the many settings by Herbert Howells, the setting composed for Winchester Cathedral by Jonathan Harvey, and the *Nunc Dimittis* by Gustav Holst).

The style of the music to which the canticles are sung,

whether simple or complex, ancient or contemporary, is a vehicle to enable the worshipper to enter into the spirit and substance of these songs. They summarise the essence of the Gospel, inviting our reflection and response to it.

# WORDS FOR REFLECTION

When Mary sings the *Magnificat*, she wants to make God look bigger, to draw attention to the greatness of God, as we do when we sing it... She has literally allowed something – someone – beyond herself, beyond her furthest imagining – to come to life in her. She is not only saying words that make God look greater; she is performing the most extraordinary and the most utterly self-forgetting action a human being could perform, making room for the life of the everlasting Word of God in her own flesh... There is more room for God, because the usual obstacles to God's work, in self-preoccupation and fear and resentment, have been overcome in Mary's unswerving willingness to absorb the vision God has given.

Rowan Williams[46]


Because of his visitation, we may no longer desire God as if he were lacking: our redemption is no longer a question of pursuit but of surrender to him who is always and everywhere present. Therefore at every moment we pray that, following him, we may depart from our anxiety into his peace.

W. H. Auden[47]


As our society has drifted further and further away from the practice of faith; so we have drifted away from recognizing the presence of God in the poor and the needy. We have become rather complacent about our values, believing that social virtue is what all nice and good people believe in and practise, that we have no need for the nourishment of common prayer … Scripture brings us to the temple, the Holy of Holies, to a God so holy that he cannot be seen, and so cannot simply be a flattering reflection of ourselves. Scripture is full of surprises. The greatest surprise is God's constant subversion of our expectations which leads to the conversion of our desires. That is why God comes to us as a baby; calling out our love and delight. But the baby Jesus will grow into a man, a man who walks beside the lakeside of our lives and calls us to follow him, to service and suffering.

Angela Tilby[48]

It is she, this little one, who leads them all.
For Faith sees only what is.
And she, she sees what will be.
Charity loves only what is.
And she, she loves what will be.
Faith sees what is.
In Time and in Eternity.
Hope sees what will be.
In time and for eternity.

Charles Péguy[49]

# 7

# THE CRIES OF OUR HEARTS

## *The Lesser Litany, Lord's Prayer, Preces and Collects*

The Lord be with you.
And with thy spirit.

Let us pray.

Lord, have mercy upon us.
Christ, have mercy upon us.
Lord, have mercy upon us.

Our Father, which art in heaven, Hallowed be thy Name,
Thy kingdom come, Thy will be done, in earth as it is in
heaven. Give us this day our daily bread; And forgive us our
trespasses, As we forgive them that trespass against us; And
lead us not into temptation, But deliver us from evil. Amen.

O Lord, shew thy mercy upon us.
And grant us thy salvation.
O Lord, save the Queen.
And mercifully hear us when we call upon thee.
Endue thy Ministers with righteousness.

---

And make thy chosen people joyful.
O Lord, save thy people.
And bless thine inheritance.
Give peace in our time, O Lord.
Because there is none other that fighteth for us, but only thou, O God.
O God, make clean our hearts within us.
And take not thy Holy Spirit from us.

---

AFTER HEARING AND responding to the scriptures, Evensong changes gear as the worshipper is led from praise to prayer. Up to this moment, the emphasis has been a celebration of the character of God, the recalling of God's engagement with the world and humanity's response to God. Now, our needs and desires are voiced in short, charged phrases that frame the prayer Christ gave to his followers (known almost universally as the Lord's Prayer). It reflects an insight from the worship of the Orthodox churches of the East (which Thomas Cranmer knew), that the closer we come to the glory of God, the more we recognise our need for healing, mercy and peace – both for ourselves and for the world and its peoples.

This is a pattern that also follows the monastic services on which Thomas Cranmer broadly based his forms of Morning and Evening Prayer in the first *BCP*, where the singing of the canticle was followed by the supplication that begins 'Lord, have mercy' and the Lord's Prayer. Cranmer also drew upon the forms of worship that were widely used in English cathedrals and parish churches that were not monastic foundations. In particular, the forms of worship used in Salisbury Cathedral before the Reformation (known as the Use of Sarum). This was widespread before the Reformation, where further short prayers (or *Preces* in Latin) were added after the Lord's Prayer, notably at Compline (or Night Prayer).

## PRIMAL YEARNING

The first of these prayers, beginning 'Lord, have mercy upon us' is one of the most ancient prayers that Christianity absorbed from its Jewish roots. It expresses a fundamental desire for divine mercy as we acknowledge our fears and failures. It originates in the psalms[50] and is a prayer found in the gospels.[51] It became a feature of worship from an early moment in the development of Christianity; and in the worship of the Orthodox churches of the East it is the most frequently repeated prayer.

It is known as the Lesser Litany, as it is derived from the concluding part of the longer Greater Litany (from the Latin *litania* meaning supplication), that Cranmer first wrote in 1544 and subsequently adapted for inclusion in the *Book of Common Prayer*. It follows the shape of an ancient form of prayer[52] which Cranmer adapted from litanies used in the Medieval Use of Sarum and the work of the German Reformer, Martin Luther.

The three short petitions of the Lesser Litany may, at first, seem too short, even perfunctory, to carry the weight of what we might want to express. The burden of the anxieties, disappointments and failures that we may carry personally, coupled to the panorama of suffering, destruction and brutality that dominates the news almost every day, may seem altogether too great. And yet it is in the understated simplicity of these primitive words that we are given space to articulate our longing for mercy – especially at those times when we struggle to find words of our own that might do justice to what we are feeling. To use words, however sparse, that countless masses of worshippers have used long before us, and still use persistently and repeatedly, can be extraordinarily effective – and liberating. They may provide both the spiritual energy we need to express our sorrow, and the sense of catharsis that comes with knowing that our prayer is heard.

## HUMAN NEED

The prayer that follows is the one Jesus taught his followers to use, recorded in the Gospels of Matthew (Matthew 6:9-13) and Luke (Luke 11:2-4). Almost without exception, the version in Matthew, which is longer, is the one that has been used in worship and most is most widely known. Its earliest recorded use in Christian worship dates from around the late first century CE.[53]

Since that time, successive scholars and preachers have sought to unfold the meaning of this prayer.[54] It is a prayer that carries our desire to pray and offers a shape to our own praying. In a significant sense, it is a prayer that reflects the shape and flow of Evensong. It begins by focussing on God and the character of God; inviting us to consider how challenging and renewing is life lived in company with God, and in co-operation with God's desire for the world. It then moves to address our basic human needs, as well as a longing to forgive as we believe we are forgiven; ending with the appeal that we will be strengthened to resist evil and be protected from it.

## SALVATION AND SOCIETY

The Lord's Prayer is followed by the Preces: six short petitions in the form of versicles and responses, which are drawn from verses from the psalms. They summarise the prayer of the whole Church, and invite us to place our own needs and hopes alongside words that have been prayed for centuries – and are still prayed by countless unknown, unknowable people today. They reflect the Church's earliest instincts about intercessory (or asking) prayer being short, condensing our most deeply-felt needs to as few words as possible. This gently challenges the assumption that the most sincere prayers are always the most verbose. It also reflects the principle undergirding Benedictine worship, that less is more. This is modelled in one of the most recent prayers used at the Eucharist, based on one probably composed in the seventh century CE:

> Look with favour on your people
> and in your mercy hear the cry of our hearts.
> Bless the earth,
> heal the sick,
> let the oppressed go free
> and fill your Church with power from on high.[55]

At one level, these are prayers that reflect the Church's understanding of the kind of society it served at the time the *BCP* was compiled, where a desire for salvation was linked to the need for a stable and peaceable social order, centred around the rule of the monarch, along with freedom from the activities and attitudes that might undermine this sought-after stability. It is also an expression of the Church's present-day relationship to the wider society it seeks to serve, accentuating how the Church is part of contemporary political reality: as it prays for the transformation of the social sphere; and the relationships and human transactions that make for its cohesion.

## GATHERING TOGETHER

The Preces lead to the singing of three concluding prayers, known as Collects (from the Latin *Collecta* 'to gather'), that bring together into one the diverse and unspoken prayers of the people. Normally, there are three prayers to conclude this part of Evensong. The first changes weekly, or may change on a particular day if it is a festival or a saints' day. The final two are unchanging and reflect the monastic and Medieval origins of Evensong. They are translations by Thomas Cranmer of the Collects that concluded Evening Prayer (Vespers) and Night Prayer (Compline); again, reflecting how Evensong is a combining of these two monastic offices. The final one is especially evocative of worship at the close of day, and has become one of the best loved prayers in the Anglican tradition:

> Lighten our darkness, we beseech thee, O Lord;
> and by thy great mercy defend us from all perils and
> dangers of this night; for the love of thy only Son,
> our Saviour Jesus Christ. Amen.

These are structured prayers, and follow a pattern that was probably well-established by at least the Fourth century.[56] In the monastic tradition (and more widely at celebrations of the Eucharist), the Collect would be introduced with an invitation to pray, followed by a period of silence for people to make their own silent prayers. Then the Collect would be sung or recited to symbolise how all prayers are being gathered up and summarised in the Church's prayer. This is just another suggestion of how our prayers are 'collected' along with those of countless people who have prayed, and continue to pray, these same words.

## WORDS FOR REFLECTION

The [Lord's Prayer] as a whole tells us we stand in a very vulnerable place. We stand in the middle of a human world where God's will is not the most automatic thing that people do. Where crisis faces us, where uncertainty is all around about tomorrow and where evil is powerfully at work. To stand with dignity and freedom in a world like that, we need to know that God is Our Father. We need to know that whatever happens to us God is God, God's name and presence and power and word are holy and wonderful … With that confidence, that kind of unchildish dependence, we are actually free. We know that there is a relationship that nothing can break.

Rowan Williams[57]

Prayer the church's banquet, angel's age,
God's breath in man returning to his birth,
The soul in paraphrase, heart in pilgrimage,
The Christian plummet sounding heav'n and earth
Engine against th' Almighty, sinner's tow'r,
Reversed thunder, Christ-side-piercing spear,
The six-days world transposing in an hour,
A kind of tune, which all things hear and fear;
Softness, and peace, and joy, and love, and bliss,
Exalted manna, gladness of the best,
Heaven in ordinary, man well drest,
The milky way, the bird of Paradise,
Church-bells beyond the stars heard, the soul's blood,
The land of spices; something understood.

George Herbert[58]

After this our Lord shewed concerning Prayer. In which Shewing I see two conditions in our Lord's signifying: one is rightfulness, another is sure trust. But yet oftentimes our trust is not full: for we are not sure that God heareth us, as we think because of our unworthiness, and because we feel right nought, (for we are as barren and dry oftentimes after our prayers as we were afore); and this, in our feeling our folly, is cause of our weakness. For thus have I felt in myself. And all this brought our Lord suddenly to my mind, and shewed these words, and said: *I am Ground of thy beseeching: first it*

*is my will that thou have it; and after, I make thee to will it;*
*and after, I make thee to beseech it and thou beseechest it. How*
*should it then be that thou shouldst not have thy beseeching?*

Julian of Norwich[59]

It seems to me that the soul … uses only a small number of
words, none of them extraordinary. This is how one recognises
that there *is* a soul at that moment, if at the same time one
experiences the sensation that everything else – everything
that would require a larger vocabulary – is mere possibility.

Paul Valéry[60]

# 8

# UNTOLD LAMENT
# AND UNFETTERED
# PRAISE

## *The Anthem*

FOR MANY WORSHIPPERS, the singing of the anthem is a high-point of Choral Evensong. It provides a space for reflection, and even enjoyment, when the music surrounds our thankfulness or sorrow, nourishing our hopes or expressing regrets; offering a moment when the feelings, concerns, or the excitement we bring with us to worship can be enlarged through the music the choir is singing. It is a time in the service, more than any other, when we are simply given the gift of a composer's creativity, the skill and discipline of the choir and organist in giving life to the notes on the page, and are encouraged to make it part of our own, silent offering as we share its beauty with others who are present.

## HISTORY AND STYLE

Each cathedral, college and church choir will have literally hundreds of anthems in its repertoire. In a short guide such as this, it is not possible to provide a comprehensive survey of each and every anthem that may be sung at Evensong, not least because each cathedral or church will probably have a repertoire that is unique and distinctive, including works by composers associated with that place (past and present).

Some anthems will have been composed as long ago as the early fifteenth century (and possibly even earlier) and span the course of subsequent centuries up to the present day. Each period has its own distinctive musical style, and each composer their own unique voice. Anthems composed before the Reformation to Latin texts will include music by composers such as John Taverner (c.1490-1545), Thomas Tallis or John Sheppard (c.1515-1558). It is often highly florid, based on plainsong, surrounding us in a great 'wash' of sound, that reflects the vast and decorative spaces in which it is often sung. Similar things could be said of the music of European composers from the same period such as Jean Mouton (1459-1522), Orlando Lassus (c. 1530-1594) and Josquin des Prez (c. 1450-1521). Here, the words of the anthem are less important than the desire to evoke the transcendent dimension of the worship being offered. Their Counter-Reformation successors, Giovanni Pierluigi da Palestrina (1525-94) and Tomás Luis de Victoria (1548-1611), produced no less elaborate polyphony but also sought to express the text with greater clarity. Music composed in England after the Reformation (by Orlando Gibbons, Thomas Tomkins and Thomas Weelkes, as well as settings of texts in English by Thomas Tallis and William Byrd) is more direct, with a greater emphasis on articulating the words. At the time of the first *Book of Common Prayer*, Thomas Cranmer and his fellow reformers had stipulated that musical settings should be simple, with only one note to every syllable of the text, in contrast to the ornate, pre-Reformation settings. This reflected the concern that the text (which was almost exclusively drawn from the Bible) should be clearly accessible and understood.

# TRADITION AND INNOVATION

This is a principle that tended to be followed in subsequent centuries by composers such as John Blow, Henry Purcell, and Samuel Sebastian Wesley. To achieve a more expansive musical style, they would often repeat words in order to create satisfying musical phrases. Towards the end of the nineteenth century, figures such as Hubert Parry (1848-1918) and Charles Villiers Stanford, employed a more structured musical form, giving their church music the same disciplined attention as they did their symphonies and chamber music. This was significant in raising standards after a period of malaise during the late eighteenth and early nineteenth centuries. It was also a time when composers were given greater flexibility to set texts for worship from sources other than the Bible, such as hymns or poetry that expressed Christian beliefs. For example, Stanford's Easter anthem *When Mary through the Garden Went* is a work that sets a poem by Mary Coleridge, which is a dramatically sensitive depiction of Mary Magdalene's search for Jesus on Easter morning.

During the twentieth century, the next generation of composers would produce music that extended and even challenged previous conventions. Notably, Herbert Howells' distinctive voice combined impressionistic harmony with the long musical lines that were a feature before the Reformation. In his anthems and canticle settings, words and syllables are given many notes in order to create a soaring (even sensuous) musical impact. The closing section of his 1941 anthem *Like as the hart desireth the waterbrooks* is a particularly memorable example.

Since the 1960s, composers have been even more adventurous and experimental in their musical language. Cathedral organists from this period such as Arthur Wills (1926-2020) and, from a later generation, David Briggs (b.

1962), have drawn heavily on the dissonant musical language of the French organ tradition. Two contrasting approaches may be found in the work of Jonathan Harvey (1939-2012) who was influenced by the so-called 'serial' movement, and employed electronic elements in his music; and John Tavener (1944-2013) whose mature works draw heavily on the traditional chants of the Orthodox churches to create a mystical, ethereal impact. Alongside more challenging musical language from the late twentieth and twenty-first centuries, the music of composers such as Malcolm Archer (b. 1952), John Rutter (b. 1945) and Richard Shephard (1949-2021), while always distinctive and original, tends towards a more accessible means of musical expression. In particular, many of John Rutter's Christmas carols, and his anthem *God be in my head*, have become much-loved features of the choral repertoire.

## LINGUISTIC DIVERSITY
One notable development over the past half-century is the greater freedom to sing anthems, particularly works by European composers, in their original language – noticeably Latin which had been proscribed in Anglican worship since the Reformation. Earlier in the twentieth century, if an anthem had been composed by a European composer, the original text would have been translated into English, to reflect the reformers' concern that all worship should be offered in the vernacular. Today, there is an instinctive and widespread openness to the enriching dimension of different cultural, linguistic and theological perspectives. An anthem sung at Choral Evensong is just as likely to have been composed originally for Roman Catholic, Orthodox or Lutheran services, originally set to a Latin, German, French or Slavonic text. This is one way of signifying the degree to which different Christian churches are working

together to achieve reconciliation after the bitter disputes of past centuries, and how music can be a powerful dimension in this process of healing and seeking consensus.

## ANCIENT AND MODERN TENDENCIES

Until the late nineteenth and early twentieth centuries, anthems composed for the English choral tradition were almost exclusively settings of words from the scriptures. There are some notable exceptions from the Jacobean period, such as Orlando Gibbons' *See, see the word is incarnate* that sets a narrative poem by the seventeenth-century Bishop of Gloucester, Godfrey Goodman, tracing the life of Christ from birth to resurrection and ascension. Thomas Tomkins's *Above the stars my sweet Saviour dwells* sets an Advent poem by the mid-seventeenth-century Bishop of Norwich, Joseph Hall. In order to create variety and contrast in the texts of anthems, many composers from the eighteenth century onwards used a collage of biblical texts from Old and New Testaments within the one anthem. Samuel Sebastian Wesley's oft-sung Easter anthem *Blessed be the God and Father* is a notable example, as is Philip Moore's 1980 anthem *All Wisdom Commeth from the Lord*.

It is not until the early twentieth century that composers explored a wider literary canon for words to set as anthems, as they were able to draw on a movement of rediscovery of long-forgotten texts from the Middle Ages and the Elizabethan and Jacobean periods. Composers such as Ralph Vaughan Williams (who had discovered many of these texts as part of his involvement in projects such as *The Oxford Book of Carols* and the *English Hymnal*) along with Gustav Holst (1874-1934) and Edmund Rubbra (1901-1986) are notable examples. Benjamin Britten's magical sequence for treble voices and harp *A Ceremony of Carols* reflects this tendency; as does Gerald Finzi's frequent choice of poems from the seventeenth century. Richard Crashaw's poem (which draws on the hymns of the thirteenth-century theologian Thomas Aquinas) was used by Finzi for his 1946 anthem *Lo, the full final sacrifice*. The oft-heard anthems of William H. Harris (1883-1973) such as *Faire is the Heaven*, setting words by Edmund Spencer (*c.* 1552-99) and *Bring us, O Lord God*, a setting of a prayer based on words by John Donne (1572-1631) are further examples. More recently, Gabriel Jackson (b. 1961) chose to juxtapose words by the seventeenth-century Welsh priest and poet, Henry Vaughan, with those of the twentieth and twenty-first-century poet, Geoffrey Hill, for his 2005 anthem *A Deep but Dazzling Darkness* composed for St Paul's Cathedral.

One significant outcome of late-nineteenth and early twentieth-century research into earlier literature is that composers have been drawn to set words that emphasise the role of Mary in the narrative of salvation. In the period immediately after the sixteenth-century Reformation, this would have been unthinkable: Mary and the saints were the focus of the reformers' antagonism towards Medieval devotional practices. In the wake of the nineteenth-century Tractarian Movement, as well as the momentum of the Gothic Revival, and coupled to the literary research that followed in its wake, composers seized on recently rediscovered texts that ignited their imagination. For example, settings of the Medieval poem *I sing of a maiden* proliferated in the early twentieth century, notably by Patrick Hadley (1899-1973) and Arnold Bax (1883-1953). In a further development, music arising from the Orthodox tradition is gaining popularity, notably settings by John Tavener; as well as the iconic *Bogoroditse Devo* (Hail, Mary, full of grace) from the All-Night Vigil of Sergei

Rachmaninoff (1873-1943). This has enabled the regular performance of music at Evensong, especially during the period from Advent to Candlemas, dating from the early Middle Ages to the present day, that echoes the spirit of the *Magnificat* in recognising the significance of Mary in the devotional and theological tradition of Christians.

## TIMES AND SEASONS

Great care is taken to choose a suitable anthem to reflect the season of the year, or the festival being celebrated that day, the time of day, or maybe to amplify the readings that have been heard earlier in the service. This is why, if you worship at Choral Evensong during the season of Lent that precedes Easter, for example, you are more likely to hear anthems that are reflective and subdued in character, setting texts that express sorrow and penitence, with an emphasis on the greatness of God's mercy.

By contrast, over the fifty days after Easter (and the forty days following Christmas), the music is more likely to be energetic and celebratory, setting texts that echo the rejoicing of the Church at the resurrection (or the birth and manifestation) of Christ. This is a time when 'alleluia' is an oft-repeated refrain. At any time of the year, you are likely to hear anthems, especially at mid-week services, that have a quiet and serene character, reflecting the valedictory tone of worship offered at the close of day. This is when you might hear settings of words drawn from the Medieval (or earlier) services of Evening and Night Prayer, such as Thomas Tallis's *Te lucis ante terminum* (a setting of the traditional hymn from Compline), John Sheppard's *In manus tuas* (again from Compline, a setting of the words 'into your hands, O Lord, I commend my spirit'), or Charles Wood's *Hail, gladdening light*, with its restful middle section that sets the words 'now we are come to sun's hour of rest.'

# HISTORICAL CHANCE
Today, the anthem may be a treasured moment in the overall flow of Choral Evensong, but it is a part of the service that remains because of an accident of history, reflecting the distinctive pattern of daily prayer that emerged in England after the Reformation. Originally, especially in the earlier monastic tradition, the service ended with the final prayer (or Collect). At evening or Night Prayer, an additional hymn (or antiphon) may have been sung in plainsong in honour of the Blessed Virgin Mary by way of conclusion. In cathedrals and colleges, this ending to the service was often an occasion to sing an elaborate setting of one of the traditional Latin texts in honour of Mary[61] and was often one of the most popular acts of worship in the late-Middle Ages.[62]

When Cranmer compiled the first *Book of Common Prayer*, he added a rubric after the final Collect at both Morning and Evening Prayer: 'in quires and places where they sing, here followeth the anthem.' This is just one indication that the English reformers were more conservative than some of their European counterparts and did not seek to disband the choral foundations in cathedrals, colleges and major parish churches. In this, they may have had active encouragement from keen musical monarchs such as Henry VIII and Elizabeth I. Elsewhere in Europe, especially in parts of Switzerland, The Netherlands, Scotland and (what is now) Eastern France, choirs were dissolved in favour of purely congregational singing, usually metrical versions of the psalms.

Cranmer may have recognised that this substantial musical element in the Medieval services was a popular part of worship in cathedrals. It was an opportunity that composers grasped with creativity and imagination, working positively with the constraints imposed by the reformers, enabling us to continue to enjoy their work today and for our worship to be enriched and enlarged by it.

## ENJOYMENT AND ENRICHMENT

To be able to enjoy this level of musical creativity is an aspect of worship that should be cherished and celebrated. It may be true that the reformers of the sixteenth century saw music as valuable insofar as it was a device to transmit the Bible in English, which is a position still broadly maintained by some theologians.[63] However, it was the more radical reformers of the mid-seventeenth century who discerned that our noblest human instinct is 'to glorify God, and to enjoy him forever.'[64] In that sense, we are invited to discern how all God's gifts in creation can be enjoyed for their own sake, as gifts freely given, without becoming anxious about how they are expressing a particular cultural or theological stance. This inevitably encourages us to simply enjoy God in worship, without any preconditions, as an expression of our openness to the one who is beyond control and containment.[65]

There will be times when we will bring to worship a measure of sorrow that longs for consolation or a depth of grieving for which we need to lament, as well as barely contained exhilaration or relieved gratitude that calls for an expression of delight and celebration. The music of the anthem at Evensong can be a crucial means of expressing those aspects of our lives for which words seem elusive or inadequate. This can be a means of realising an insight at the heart of the New Testament:

> We do not know how to pray as we ought, but the Spirit himself intercedes for us with sighs too deep for words. And God, who searches the heart, knows what is the mind of the Spirit, because the Spirit pleads for God's own people in God's own way.[66]

## MAKING IT PERSONAL

In conclusion, one fruitful way of hearing and engaging with the music of the anthem might be to acquire an awareness of how the music (as well as the composer's response to the text) often arises out of the very human exigencies and opportunities in a composer's life. This often imparts its own integrity to the praise or lament being expressed. For example, some of the Latin texts set by William Byrd (1540-1623), such as *Civitas sancti tuae* and *Ave verum corpus* arise from the deep sense of exile he felt as a devout Catholic, living at a time when the Reformation was being implemented in England and Catholic worship was, potentially, punishable by death. The well-documented intensity of the grief that informed the music of Herbert Howells[67] after the death of his nine year-old son, Michael, is implicit in most of his choral music, even at its most passionate and sensual. It is especially evident in his *Requiem* of 1936; as well as his 1961 *Sequence for St Michael* that begins with two heart-rending cries of 'Michael'!

By contrast, the positive, vivacious personality of a composer like William Mathias is unmistakable in works such as his 1973 anthem *Lift up your heads* and the royal wedding anthem of 1979 *Let the people praise thee, O God*. Similar things could be said about the music of Benjamin Britten (his *Jubilate* of 1961, for example) and Kenneth Leighton, who combines sinuous lines of counterpoint with ecstatic bursts of praise in an anthem such as *God's Grandeur*, his 1962 setting of Gerard Manley Hopkins's poem of the same title.

Very often, the date of an anthem's composition may be a clue to the events that were the backdrop to its creation. John Ireland's remembrance anthem of 1912, *Greater love hath no man*, opens with words from the Song of Songs ('Many waters cannot quench love') which can only have been a response to the sinking of the Titanic in the same year. Charles Villiers Stanford, whose music is often symbolic of the certainties of British imperialism, introduces a degree of questioning (after a dramatic beginning) in his setting of words from the Hebrew prophecy of Habakkuk *For lo, I raise up*, composed at the start of the First World War in 1914. In a similar vein, the music of the Estonian composer, Arvo Pärt (b. 1935) is informed by the Soviet suppression of religious expression that overshadowed the first half-century and more of his life. It is as much a sub-text in more recent works such as *The Deer's Cry* (2007) as well as the earlier *Beatitudes* (1990).

Obviously, it is never necessary to come to Evensong armed with an in-built encyclopaedia of musical biography and history. Nonetheless, a growing familiarity with the repertoire of anthems can be enriched by an awareness of the music's broader context. Just as the biblical readings (and the psalms) sung at Evensong have emerged from different times and cultures, and express distinct human and social circumstances; so the music has emerged both as an articulation of the composer's personality as well as the environment in which their work has been composed. This, in turn, can be one way of allowing the music to speak to us.

# WORDS FOR REFLECTION

But let my due feet never fail
To walk the studious cloister's pale,
And love the high embowed roof,
With antique pillars massy proof,
And storied windows richly dight,
Casting a dim religious light.
There let the pealing organ blow,
To the full-voic'd quire below,

In service high, and anthems clear,
As may with sweetness, through mine ear,
Dissolve me into ecstasies,
And bring all Heav'n before mine eyes.

John Milton[68]

When music speaks wordlessly like an illumination, people know they are receiving, not imposing, its meaning ... The music comes out to meet them and address them as an 'other', and nothing can persuade them that they are looking merely at their own feelings reflected in a mirror.

John V. Taylor[69]

From harmony, from Heav'nly harmony
This universal frame began.
When Nature underneath a heap
Of jarring atoms lay,
And could not heave her head,
The tuneful voice was heard from high,
Arise ye more than dead.
Then cold, and hot, and moist, and dry,
In order to their stations leap,
And music's pow'r obey.
From harmony, from Heav'nly harmony
This universal frame began:
From harmony to harmony
Through all the compass of the notes it ran,
The diapason closing full in man.

John Dryden[70]

Je crois en Dieu qui chante     *I believe in God who sings*
Et qui fait chanter la vie.     *and who makes life itself to sing.*

Noel Colombier[71]

# 9

# SOUNDING THE DEPTHS

## *The Prayers of Intercession, Final Hymn and Blessing*

MUCH OF THE form and content of Choral Evensong has an objective character. Its lack of specificity makes it all-embracing. Its words can express a wide range of hope, sorrow, joy and thankfulness. In that sense, little more needs to be added to what has already been said and sung. We have placed the things on our hearts and minds alongside the words of the service and the music with which it has been clothed. It has all been gathered up into the on-going momentum of the Church's endless stream of prayer and praise.

Nonetheless, we come to worship not as anonymous cogs in the machinery of a vast, impersonal universe. We are people with needs and desires that are unique and specific, and we live our lives as part of a network of relationships where we are aware of the longings and hopes of others. We are also part of a world that is as complex as it is fragile, where there has not been one single day of peace for as long as anyone can remember, and where immense suffering and injustice happens at the same time as immeasurable acts of love and compassion. Above all else, we are created as unique individuals in the image and likeness of God, who hears us, attends to us, and loves us.

# A VAST OCEAN

The prayers following the anthem provide worshippers with a moment of focussed attention, where the needs, anxieties, and the things for which are most grateful in life can be articulated. This is where the focus of Evensong becomes specific. In many cathedrals this is often an opportunity to voice the prayers that visitors have left that day, maybe after lighting a candle. Along with the reading from Scripture, this is the only part of the service that involves extended speech. Most clergy responsible for this dimension of the worship will be sensitive to the fact that the whole service has been an act of prayer and praise. They will choose (and craft) their words carefully to resonate with the rest of the liturgy, recognising the need for the spoken prayers to be in proportion to the prayers that have already been sung, without creating an imbalance by overloading this closing part of the worship with too many words.

Prayers are offered for the Church, both locally and globally, to acknowledge that Christian faith and identity binds us to everyone within the body of Christ. Equally, prayers are offered for the world, for those with political responsibility, and for those suffering from the consequences of the abuse of that responsibility, as well as war, persecution, or natural and ecological disasters. There may be issues of local concern voiced in these prayers, as well as the needs of the sick and suffering, and those who have died. There is often a moment where we are given the space to silently name the people and the matters we have brought with us to worship.

# PRAYING AND BELIEVING

Sometimes, it may seem as if that the pains of the world, the needs of those we love, as well as our own hopes and fears, are simply too great and that a relatively short time of prayer is not enough to enable us to adequately name what is on our hearts and minds. This is when our desire to pray and our understanding of God come face-to-face. When we question whether our words can make any difference, as a sense of helplessness begins to overshadow us, or even frustration that there is not enough time to say all we want to say, that is often the moment when we have to allow God to be God – rather than a projection of the limits of our imagination. There is always a temptation to confine God, to limit God's unbounded freedom to do something new, to box God in by our own faltering and static definitions. But God is always much more than our definitions, or our attempts to restrict God to no more than the limits of what we can imagine or conceive. This is when it is good to remind (and reassure) ourselves that this is not a me-centred world, and that God is that 'wild and lovely power'[72] who releases us from our limitations. It enables us to make our prayers part of the vast ocean of prayer that the Church offers in every time and place, as we place our desires alongside God's desire for the wholeness of creation and every human life.

It also invites us to trust that God, who is always and everywhere present, is attentive to the particularity of our hopes and fears, even if we struggle to articulate our prayer, or our ability to imagine how this might be possible is taken to its furthest limits. At one level, we are simply invited to trust that our own prayers can be gathered up into the great love that holds all of life and death together, as it becomes part of God's continual self-giving for the world and its peoples. As one poet discerned, in the lonely hours of darkness:

There are nights that are so still
that I can hear the small owl calling
far off and a fox barking
miles away. It is then that I lie
in the lean hours awake listening
to the swell born somewhere in the Atlantic
rising and falling, rising and falling
wave on wave on the long shore
by the village, that is without light
and companionless. And the thought comes
of that other being who is awake, too,
letting our prayers break on him,
not like this for a few hours,
but for days, years, for eternity.[73]

# FINDING A VOICE TO PRAISE

At weekends and on festivals, Evensong usually ends with a hymn sung by everyone present. This is an opportunity to use our singing voice to contribute to worship that has, until now, invited us to be attentive and involved by listening and looking. This can be a moment of release, when we join our voice to that of the choir and clergy who have been singing the service, to allow a distinctive and individual feature of our unique identity to be heard as part of the greater sound of rejoicing, sorrow, or hope. After being still and silent for a significant period of time, the physical sensation of singing, with the need to inhale and exhale breath in an exaggerated way, can be quite striking. When we sing, we can *feel* the difference – as well as hear it. If our praying can be part of God's own self-giving, our singing is equally a moment when our physical and mental energy becomes focussed and projected into a larger arena of prayer and praise. Even if we have convinced ourselves (or others have misled us by telling us) that we cannot sing very well, what we give of ourselves at this moment is a significant element in the overall sound. Without my voice, the sound would not be the same and this moment of the worship would lack something vital.

The hymn chosen to conclude Evensong will usually reflect the season of the year, the festival being celebrated, or the time of day. During the more reflective, expectant and penitential seasons, such as Advent and Lent, it is more likely to be a hymn of hope or of sorrow. During the extended periods of celebration after Christmas and Easter, the hymn is more likely to have a jubilant emphasis.

Very often, hymns can be an important way of expressing not only our own feelings, hopes and concerns; they can provide a poetic summary of what Christians believe by expressing the emerging and developing faith of the Church. It has often been said that hymns provide worshippers with a means to 'do theology' – to voice something of the vastness of the words and thinking that has attempted to make sense of God and life for many millennia. Very often, if you want an insight into the experience and insights of Christians from previous generations, and how they can enrich our own, the dates of a hymn-writer's life can tell you a great deal about the emphases of faith at that time.

## PARTING GIFTS

The hymn is usually followed by a blessing. This mirrors the Trinitarian song of praise with which Evensong began. It is a significant moment, as we are assured that God the Father, the Son and the Holy Spirit is with us, to sustain us and surround us as we leave worship. It might be helpful to recognise it as a moment of 'handing over', as the things we have received during the course of Evensong are given to us to take away, to make a difference in a world of competing demands and opportunities. It is an invitation to give a small part of the beauty, harmony and stillness we have absorbed to our ordinary routines and human encounters, especially when they seem unattractive, dissonant and frenetic.

The final part of Evensong will be the organ voluntary (except, perhaps, on those Fridays when Evensong is unaccompanied in most cathedrals and chapels). This conclusion is an invitation to be attentive to the artistry of the composer as much as the skill of the organist in bringing the music to life. Whether it is a 'big' showpiece such as a work by a nineteenth or early-twentieth-century French composer such as Widor or Guilmant, or an exquisite miniature such one of J. S. Bach's profound chorale-preludes, it is a moment to savour. It is not only the outcome of a composer's inspiration and creative imagination; but years of disciplined study – by both the composer as well as the organist. It is not audio wallpaper over which we thoughtlessly talk and chatter, but a final parting gift to cherish until we next come to worship, as our lives continue and, little by little, reflect what we have received.

# WORDS FOR REFLECTION

Prayer is the flower of gentleness and of freedom from anger. Prayer is the fruit of joy and thankfulness. Prayer is the remedy for gloom and despondency. Do not pray that your own will may be done, for your will may not accord with the will of God. But pray as you have been taught, saying: Thy will be done in me. Pray to him in this way about everything – that his will be done. For he desires what is good and profitable for your soul, whereas you do not always ask for this. Often in my prayers I have asked for what I thought was good, and persisted in my petition, stupidly trying to force the will of God, instead of leaving it to him to arrange things as he knows best. But afterwards, on obtaining what I asked for, I was very sorry that I did not pray rather for God's will to be done; because the thing turned out to be different from what I expected… Strive never to pray against anyone. If when you are praying no other joy can attract you, then truly you have found prayer.

Evagrius of Pontus[74]

Prayer is not asking God to get things done in the way we think best: that amounts merely to another trick in the power game. Nor is true prayer a petition for special guidance, which can often be a form of one-upmanship. And prayer most certainly does not consist of 'worrying on my knees' which usually only makes me more confused. To pray is to place oneself in the silent presence of the Eternal Beyond, the God of truth and love, and letting the flow of communication between that and one's truest self clarify the distorted vision, purify the motives, countervail the pressures and set one free from dependence upon any other power except the care for others which holds on, trusting, hoping and enduring, until in the long term it wins through.

John V. Taylor[75]

Everyone suddenly burst out singing:
And I was filled with such delight
As prisoned birds must find in freedom,
Winging wildly across the white
Orchards and dark-green fields: on – on – and out of sight.

Everyone's voice was suddenly lifted;
And beauty came like the setting sun;
My heart was shaken with tears: and horror
Drifted away . . . O, but Everyone
Was a bird; and the song was wordless; the singing will
     never be done.

Siegfried Sassoon[76]

Praise with your whole selves: that is, let not your tongue and voice alone praise God, but... your deeds. For now, when we are gathered together in the Church, we praise: when we go forth each to our own business, we seem to cease to praise God. Let us not cease to live well, and then we will ever praise God... Attend not only to the sound; when you praise God, praise with your whole selves: let your voice, your life, your deeds, all sing.

Augustine of Hippo[77]

# 10

# CHANCING UPON GLORY

## *Quires and Places where they Sing*

CHORAL EVENSONG AND other forms of choral worship are offered in all the Church of England's cathedrals, in major parish churches and in the chapels of colleges and schools. Some Roman Catholic cathedrals regularly sing a choral form of Vespers (or Evening Prayer), notably Westminster Cathedral, which had been home to one of England's finest choirs. Choral services take place in some monastic communities that have schools (e.g. Ampleforth and Worth Abbeys). Except in some schools, these services are freely open to anyone who wishes to join the worship.

Each of the Church of England's cathedrals has its own website, where detailed service schedules can be accessed, giving the times of services and the music being sung. Since the COVID-19 pandemic necessitated either the closure of churches for public worship, or restrictions on the numbers of people attending worship for extended periods, most of the Church of England's cathedrals and many of its larger churches, along with some chapels of Cambridge and Oxford colleges, have made the livestreaming and webcasting of services a permanent feature of their schedules. Beyond the Church of England, the following is just a small selection of Anglican cathedrals and churches that have well-established livestreaming and webcasting facilities via their websites:

- St Fin Barre's Cathedral, Cork
- Christ Church Cathedral, Dublin
- St Patrick's Cathedral, Dublin
- St Mary's Cathedral, Edinburgh
- St Thomas Church, Fifth Avenue, New York City
- Washington National Cathedral

These broadcasts can be a helpful way of becoming familiar with the shape and content of Choral Evensong, as well gaining confidence about what to expect before attending in person. However, there is no substitute for being present in-person and experiencing the words and music in their physical, architectural setting, joining the stream of worship that has been offered in that place over the course of centuries.

The following websites also provide details of services in most cathedrals, major churches and colleges:

**Cathedral Music Trust** is a voice for cathedral music, campaigning on behalf of cathedral music and musicians, supporting choirs and choristers in need, and encouraging the pursuit of excellence in choral and organ music. Its website has comprehensive links to most places where Choral Evensong is regularly sung across the British Isles and links to their websites.

www.cathedralmusictrust.org.uk

**Choral Evensong** is a dedicated website that provides up-to-date information on where Choral Evensong is taking place, week-by-week, across the British Isles and beyond, with an interactive map and search facility, providing links to current service schedules. Most weeks it lists around 700 acts of worship.

https://www.choralevensong.org/uk/

**BBC Choral Evensong** Since 1927 the BBC has broadcast Choral Evensong live from a cathedral, church or chapel each week (and more recently included recorded and archived programmes). Currently, it is broadcast every Wednesday afternoon on BBC Radio 3 (and usually repeated the following Sunday).

https://www.bbc.co.uk/programmes/b006tp7r

**Archive of Recorded Church Music** is a remarkable – and growing – collection of radio and television broadcasts from 1902 onwards, along with commercial and private recordings. It includes many BBC Choral Evensong broadcasts prior to 2000 and has a dedicated YouTube channel.

https://www.recordedchurchmusic.org/

# SUGGESTIONS FOR FURTHER READING

THIS BOOK HAS offered a brief introduction to an act of worship with a long and intricate tradition. It cannot tell the whole story of how Evensong has come to be and is celebrated today. The following suggestions point the reader to more detailed information that will amplify the history of the origins and development of Evensong, as well as the theology, spirituality and music underpinning its various elements.

**General**

Bradshaw, Jones, Wainwright and Yarnold (eds.), *The Study of Liturgy*, London, SPCK, 1992, especially pp. 399-454.

Cumming (ed), *The Book of Common Prayer: The Texts of 1549, 1559, and 1662* Oxford, Oxford University Press, 2011.

Robert F. Taft, *The Liturgy of the Hours in East And West*, Collegeville, The Liturgical Press, 1993, especially chapters 18-22.

Wainwright and Westefield-Tucker (eds.), *The Oxford History of Christian Worship*, Oxford, Oxford University Press, 2005, especially Chapter 16.

**Cathedral Music**

Trevor Beeson, *In Tuneful Accord: the Church Musicians*, London, SCM Press, 2009.

Kenneth R. Long, *The Music of the English Church*, London, Hodder & Stoughton, 1991.

Martin Thomas, *English Cathedral Music and Liturgy in the Twentieth Century*, London, SCM Press, 2015.

**The Psalms**

Walter Brueggemann, *The Message of the Psalms: A Theological Commentary*, Minneapolis, Augsburg, 1984.

Michael Sadgrove, *I Will Trust in You: A Companion to the Evening Psalms*, London, SPCK, 2009.

**The Bible**

John Barton, *People of the Book?: The Authority of the Bible in Christianity*, London, SPCK, 1988.

Henry Wansbrough, *The Story of the Bible: How it Came to Us,* London, Darton, Longman and Todd, 2006.

Frances M. Young, *Brokenness and Blessing: Towards a Biblical Spirituality*, London, Darton, Longman and Todd, 2007.

**Cathedrals**

Christopher Lewis and Stephen Platten (eds.) *Flagships of the Spirit: Cathedrals and their Mission*, London, Darton, Longman and Todd, 1998.

Christopher Lewis and Stephen Platten (eds.) *Dreaming Spires?: Cathedrals in a New Age*, London, SPCK, 2006.

# SUGGESTIONS FOR FURTHER READING

Stephen Platten, *Holy Ground: Cathedrals in the Twenty-First Century*, Durham, Sacristy Press, 2017.

Robert Scott, *The Gothic Enterprise: A Guide to Understanding the Medieval Cathedral*, Berkeley, California University Press, 2003.

Christopher Somerville, *Ships of Heaven: The Private Life of Britain's Cathedrals*, London, Penguin/Doubleday, 2019.

# NOTES

1. From an introduction to a televised broadcast of Choral Evensong from York Minster, BBC2, 16 October 1996.

2. Philip Toynbee, 'Evensong at Peterborough' in *Encounter*, October 1978, pp. 121-127.

3. John Drury, 'Introduction' to *Orders of Service*, Cambridge, King's College, 1986.

4. Rowan Williams, *Lost Icons: Reflections on Cultural Bereavement*, Edinburgh, T&T Clark, 2000, p. 24.

5. Translated from the Greek by John Keble from *Common Praise*, Norwich, Hymns Ancient & Modern, 2000, 17.

6. The ancient practice of interpreting the psalms with reference to Christ's saving work has been recovered in the short optional prayers that conclude each psalm in the Church of England's most recent revision of these services in *Common Worship: Daily Prayer*, London, Church House Publishing, 2005.

7. It is adapted from the writings of Prospero of Aquitaine (c. 390-455 CE).

8. Colm Luibheid (ed.), *John Cassian Conferences* (Classics of Western Spirituality), London, SPCK, 1985, Conference 10.

9. Caroline White (ed. and trs.) *The Rule of St Benedict*, London, Penguin, 2008, Chapters 8-19

10. The Church of England's most recent revision of its worship has reverted to the more ancient monastic practice, with the first couplet being used only at Morning Prayer, and the second used at Prayer During the Day, Evening Prayer and Night Prayer. See *Common Worship: Daily Prayer*, London, Church House Publishing, 2005.

11. For example, Esther de Waal, *A Life Giving Way: A Commentary on the Rule of St Benedict*, London, Bloomsbury, 1995, p. 77.

12. The first possible mention of its use is found in the Apostolic Constitutions c. 380 CE (see Robert F. Taft, *The Liturgy of the Hours in East and West: The Origins of the Divine Office and its Meaning for Today*, Collegeville, The Liturgical Press, 1986, p. 45).

13. For example, reference is made in *Itinerarium Egeriae* (c. 380 CE), Chapter 24.

14. *Common Worship: Daily Prayer* follows more closely the ancient practice of using 'Alleluia' at this point in the service.

15. Catherine LaCugna, *God for Us: The Trinity and Christian Life*, New York, HarperCollins, 1992, p. 339.

16. 'Pied Beauty' in Catherine Philips (ed.), *Gerard Manley Hopkins, Selected Poetry*, Oxford, Oxford University Press, 1986.

17. Nicholas Ayo, *Gloria Patri: The History and Theology of the Lesser Doxology*, Indiana, University of Notre Dame Press, 2007, p. 9.

18. From a sermon preached at the National Pilgrimage, Walsingham, 2004.

19. Dietrich Bonhoeffer, *Psalms: The Prayer Book of the Bible*, Minneapolis, Augsburg Fortress, 1970.

20. Principally in the books of the Chronicles, the books of Samuel, the First book of the Kings, as well as the Psalms.

21. See, for example, Enid B. Mellor (ed.), *The Making of the Old Testament*, Cambridge, CUP, 1972, p. 32ff.

22. T.M. Horner, Herman Gunkel (eds.), *The Psalms: A Form-Critical Introduction*, Philadelphia, Fortress, 1967.

23. See, for example, Robert Taft, *The Liturgy of the Hours in East and West: The Origins of the Divine Office and Its Meaning for Today*, Collegeville, Liturgical Press, 1986, p. 31ff.

24. A good introduction to the history and musical development of Anglican chant can be found in John Scott (ed.), *The New St Paul's Cathedral Psalter*, Norwich, Canterbury Press, 1997.

25. See, for example, Walter Brueggemann, *Praying the Psalms: Engaging Scripture and the Life of the Spirit*, Oregon, Wipf and Stock, 2007.

26. Walter Brueggemann, *The Message of the Psalms: A Theological Commentary*, Minneapolis, Augsburg, 1984, p. 15.

27. From Ann Griffiths (1776-1805) 'Rhyffed, rhyffed gan angylion' cited in E. Wyn Jenkins *Flame in the Mountains: Williams Pantycelyn, Ann Griffiths and the Welsh Hymn*, Talybont, Y Lolfa, 2017.

28. Patrick Gale, *The Whole Day Through*, London, Fourth Estate, 2009, pp. 157-8.

29. Gerard Manley Hopkins, 'I Wake and Feel the Fell of Dark, Not Day' from Catherine Philips (ed.), *Gerard Manley Hopkins, Selected Poetry*, Oxford, Oxford University Press, 1986.

30. Exposition on Psalm 150 from Maria Boulding and Boniface Ramsey (eds.), St Augustine: Expositions of the Psalms (volume 6), New York, New City Press, 2005.

31. Jeremy Taylor, *Holy Living* 1.3.

32. See, for example, *The Rule of St Benedict* chapter 4.

33. See, for example, Dairmaid MacCullough, *Reformation: Europe's House Divided 1490-1700*, London, Penguin, 2004, especially pp. 184ff. and 245ff..

34. An early statement of the incorporation of Scripture, tradition and reason as a defining characteristic of the Church of England's doctrinal position was made by Richard Hooker (1554 -1600). See, for example, his *Of the Laws of Ecclesiastical Polity* Book 5, 8:2.

35. John Barton, *People of the Book: The Authority of the Bible in Christianity*, London, SPCK, 1988, p. 3.

36. George Caird (1917-84) from *Ancient & Modern: Hymns and Songs for Refreshing Worship*, Norwich, Hymns Ancient & Modern, 2013, 738.

37. This is a pattern still followed by most Orthodox Jewish communities, although some Jewish congregations from the Reformed movement in Judaism have adopted a pattern of reading the Torah over the course of a three-year cycle.

38. Neville Clark, *Preaching in Context: Word, Worship and the People of God*, Rattlesden, Mayhew, 1991. p. 90.

39. See, for example, Michael Casey, *Sacred Reading: The Ancient Art of Lectio Divina*, Minnesota, Triumph, 1996.

40. D. W. Torrance (ed.), *John Calvin, Commentary on the Second Epistle of Paul the Apostle to the Corinthians*, Grand Rapids, Eerdmanns, 2001, p. 430.

41. Dietrich Bonhoeffer, *Life Together*, London, SCM, 1954, pp. 53-54.

42. George Herbert, 'The Holy Scriptures II' in John Drury and Victoria Moule (eds.), *The Complete Poetry of George Herbert*, London, Penguin, 2015.

43. From a sermon preached in Truro Cathedral, November 2004.

44. See Robert F. Taft, *The Liturgy of the Hours in East and West: The Origins of the Divine Office and its Meaning for Today*, Collegeville, Liturgical Press, 1986, pp. 126-128.

45. See Robert F. Taft, *The Liturgy of the Hours in East and West: The Origins of the Divine Office and its Meaning for Today*, Collegeville, Liturgical Press, 1986, pp. 45-56.

46. From a sermon preached at the National Pilgrimage, Walsingham, 2004.

47. From 'For the Time Being' in W. H. Auden, *Collected Poems*, London, Faber & Faber, 1994.

48. From the 2009 Candlemas Chevin Sermon, in St Bene't's Church, Cambridge.

49. From Charles Péguy, *Le Porche du mystère de la deuxième vertu*, Paris, Éditions Gallimard, 1929.

50. For example, psalms 6:2, 31:9, 123:3.

51. For example in Matthew 20:30 and Luke 18:13.

52. Cranmer's Litany follows the basic pattern of short petitions, followed by a choral or congregational response, that was a feature of Jewish worship, e.g. on Yom Kippur, the Day of Atonement; and prayers following this form are recorded in early Christian sources, e.g. Eusebius (d. 339 CE) The History of the Church.

53. The Didache (or The Lord's Teaching Through the Twelve Apostles to the Nations) is a Greek document, probably originating in Syria, that encourages the saying of the Lord's Prayer three times every day. See, for example, Thomas O'Loughlin, *The Didache: A Window on the Earliest Christians*, London, SPCK, 2010.

54. A more recent example is Kenneth Stevenson, *The Lord's Prayer: A Text in Tradition*, London, SCM Press, 2004.

55. Eucharist Prayer F in *Common Worship: Holy Communion*, London, Church House Publishing, 2000.

56. The earliest examples are found in the Apostolic Constitutions dating from c. 375-80 CE.

57. From 'Reflections on the Lord's Prayer', Canterbury Cathedral, 2007.

58. George Herbert, 'Prayer I' in John Drury and Victoria Moule (eds.) *The Complete Poetry of George Herbert*, London, Penguin, 2015.

59. Edmund College (ed.), *Julian of Norwich, Showings* (Chapter 41), London, SPCK (Classics of Western Spirituality), 1978.

60. Cited in W. H. Auden, *A Certain World: A Commonplace Book*, London, Faber & Faber, 1970, p. 261.

61. What remains of the sixteenth-century *Eton Choir Book* is a notable collection of late Medieval and early Tudor settings of these texts in honour of Mary, many of which have been recorded in recent years by choirs such as The Sixteen and Christ Church Cathedral, Oxford.

62. See Eamon Duffy, *The Stripping of the Altars: Traditional Religion in England*, c.1400-c.1580, New Haven, Yale, 2005, p. 256ff.

63. See for example the work of the Scottish theologian, Jeremy Begbie, notably his *Redeeming Transcendence: Bearing Witness to the Triune God*, Grand Rapids, Eerdmans, 2018.

64. Westminster Shorter Catechism, 1647.

65. This is an approach encouraged in the work of the English theologian David Brown, notably in his *God and Enchantment of Place: Reclaiming Human Experience*, Oxford, OUP, 2004.

66. Romans 8:26-27.

67. See Paul Spicer, *Herbert Howells*, Bridgend, Seren, 1998, especially Chapter 6.

68. From 'Il Penseroso' in John Leonard (ed.), *The Complete Poems of John Milton*, London, Penguin, 1998.

69. John V. Taylor, *The Christlike God*, London, SCM Press, 1992, pp. 30-31.

70. 'Song for St Cecilia's Day 1687' in *John Dryden, Selected Poems*, London, Penguin Classic, 2001.

71. From a hymn by Noel Colombier, Paul Iles (trs.).

72. From 'At Communion', Madeleine L'Engle, *The Ordering of Love: New and Collected Poems*, Colorado Springs, Waterbrook Press, 2005.

73. 'The Other' from R. S. Thomas, *Collected Poems 1945-1990*, London, Weidenfield & Nicolson, 1991.

74. Chapters on Prayer 14-16, 31-32, 103, 153.

75. John V. Taylor, *The Christ-like God*, London, SCM Press, p. 261.

76. 'Everyone Sang' from *Siegfried Sassoon, Collected Poems*, London, Faber & Faber, 2002.

77. Exposition on Psalm 148 from Maria Boulding and Boniface Ramsey (eds.), *St Augustine: Expositions of the Psalms* (volume 6), New York, New City Press, 2005.

# ACKNOWLEDGEMENTS

THE AUTHOR AND publisher are grateful to the following for permission to include copyright material in this publication:

The Archbishops' Council for extracts from *Common Worship: Services and Prayers of the Church of England.*

Trustees of the G. B. Caird Memorial Fund for extracts from the hymn 'Not far beyond the sea'.

Cambridge University Press, the Crown's patentee, for extracts from *The Book of Common Prayer.*

Curtis Brown Ltd for extracts from *For the Time Being* by W. H. Auden published by Faber & Faber.

The Very Revd Dr John Drury for extracts from the Introduction to *Orders of Service* as used in the Chapel of King's College, Cambridge.

HarperCollins for extracts from *The Whole Day Through* © Patrick Gale (Fourth Estate).

HarperCollins Religious for extracts from *God With Us* © Catherine LaCugna, 1992. Reproduced with permission.

Hymns Ancient & Modern for extracts from *The Christlike*

# ACNOWLEDGEMENTS

*God*, by John V. Taylor, Published by SCM Press © John V. Taylor, 1992, 2004.

Barbara Levy Literary Agency for 'Everyone Sang' copyright Siegfried Sassoon by kind permission of the estate of George Sassoon.

Pan Macmillan for 'The Other' from *H'm* by R. S. Thomas. Reproduced with permission by PLSClear.

The Revd Canon Angela Tilby for extracts from an unpublished sermon.

The Rt Revd Dr Rowan Williams for extracts from unpublished sermons.

The University of Notre Dame Press for extracts from *Gloria Patri* by Nicholas Ayo.

Much of the content of this book acknowledges the musicians whose skill and experience informs the daily offering of Choral Evensong in cathedrals, college chapels and larger churches. Equally, I want to recognise the contribution and dedication of musicians in countless local parish churches, who strive to set high standards by raising opportunity and aspiration among the young, often in the face of various pressures and obstructions. Among them is Stephen Lacey, formerly Director of Music at the parish church of St Andrew, Farnham, whose integrity and professionalism continues to lift the hearts, minds and spirits of so many people to encounter far greater things.

# INDEX

# INDEX

# INDEX